How
to Study the
Bible
Intentionally

Register This New Book

Benefits of Registering*

- ✓ FREE **replacements** of lost or damaged books
- ✓ FREE **audiobook** – *Pilgrim's Progress*, audiobook edition
- ✓ FREE information about new titles and other **freebies**

www.anekopress.com/new-book-registration

*See our website for requirements and limitations.

How
to Study the
Bible
Intentionally

Methods and Conditions
for Effective Bible Study

Reuben A. Torrey

We love hearing from our readers. Please contact us at www.anekopress.com/questions-comments with any questions, comments, or suggestions.

Cover Design: Jonathan Lewis

Editor: Paul Miller

Printed in the United States of America

Aneko Press

www.anekopress.com

Aneko Press, Life Sentence Publishing, and our logos are trademarks of

Life Sentence Publishing, Inc.
203 E. Birch Street
P.O. Box 652
Abbotsford, WI 54405

RELIGION / Christian Life / Spiritual Growth

Paperback ISBN: 978-1-62245-699-4

eBook ISBN: 978-1-62245-700-7

10 9 8 7 6 5 4 3 2 1

Available where books are sold

Contents

Preface

This book has been written for two reasons: first, because it seemed to be needed; second, to save the writer time and labor. Letters are constantly coming in from all over the world asking how to study the Bible. It is impossible to refuse to answer a question so important as that, but it takes much time to answer it as it should be answered. This book is written as an answer to those who have asked the question, and to those who may want to ask it. Nothing is more important for our own mental, moral, and spiritual development, or for our increase in usefulness, than Bible study. But not all Bible study is equally profitable. Some Bible study is absolutely profitless. How to study the Bible so as to get the most profit from it is a topic of immeasurable importance. The answer to the question, found in this book, has been for the most part given in addresses by me at the Chicago Bible Institute, at ministerial conferences and YMCA conventions before the summer gatherings of college students. Many people, especially ministers, who have heard these addresses have asked that they would be written down. I have promised for two years to comply with this request, but have never found time to do so until now.

Chapter 1

Introduction to Methods of Bible Study

We will first consider the most profitable methods of Bible study, and then we will look at the fundamental conditions of profitable Bible study. Many readers of this book will probably be frightened, at first, at the seeming elaborateness and difficulty of some of the methods of study suggested, but they are not as difficult as they appear.

Their practicality and effectiveness have been tested in the classroom, and not with classes made up completely of college graduates, but largely composed of people of very simple education – in some cases of almost no education. The methods do, though, require time and hard work. It must be remembered, however, that the Bible contains gold, and almost anyone is willing to dig for gold, especially if it is certain that he will find it. It is certain that one will find gold in the Bible – if he digs. As you use the methods recommended in this book, you will find your ability to do the work rapidly increasing by exercise, until you can soon do more in fifteen minutes than you could do in an hour when you started.

The first method of study suggested is exceptionally good mental training. When you have pursued this method of study for a while, your powers of observation will have been so enlivened that you will see at first glance what you previously saw only upon much study and reflection.

This method of study will also train the logical powers of your mind, cultivating habits of order, system, and classification in your intellectual processes. The power of clear, concise, and strong expression will be developed, as well. No book other than the Bible provides the opportunity for intellectual development by its study. No other book, and no other subject, will so abundantly repay careful and sincere study. The Bible is read much, but is studied very little in comparison.

It will probably be noticed by some that the first method of study suggested is practically the method now pursued in the study of nature. First you carefully analyze and study facts, and then you classify those facts. But what you will learn and discover from the Bible goes far beyond and above that of nature in excellence, beauty, thought, helpfulness, and practical use. The Bible is also far more accessible.

We cannot all be profound students of nature, but we can all be profound students of Scripture. Many otherwise uneducated people have a marvelous grasp of Bible truth. It was acquired by study. There are people who have studied little else, but who have studied the Scriptures by the hour, daily, and their resulting wisdom is the astonishment, and sometimes the dismay, of scholars and theologians.

Chapter 2

The Study of
Individual Books

The first method of Bible study that we will consider is the study of the Bible by individual books. This method of study is the most thorough, the most difficult, and the one that yields the best and most permanent results. We take it up first because, in my opinion, it should take up the greatest part of our time.

The first work to do is to select the book to study.
This is a very important matter. If you make an unfortunate selection, you may become discouraged and give up a method of study that could have been most fruitful.
A few points will be helpful to the beginner:

1. For your first book study, choose a short book. The choice of a long book to begin with will lead to discouragement in anyone but a person of rare perseverance. It will be so long before one

reaches the final results, which far more than pay for all the labor expended, that the ordinary student will give it up.

2. Choose a comparatively easy book. Some books of the Bible present weighty difficulties not to be found in other books. One will want to meet and overcome these later, but it is not a work for a beginner to set out upon. When his powers have become trained by reason of use, then he can do this successfully and satisfactorily, but if he attempts it, as so many rashly do, at the outset, he will soon find himself struggling. First Peter is a very precious book, but a few of the most difficult passages in the Bible are in it. If it were not for these difficult passages, it would be a good book to recommend to the beginner, but in view of these difficulties, it is not wise to try to make it a subject of exhaustive study until later.

3. Choose a book that is rich enough in its teaching to demonstrate the advantages of this method of study, thus producing a strong appetite for further studies of the same kind. When you have gone through one reasonably large and full book by the method of study about to be described, you will have an eagerness for it that will ensure that you will somehow find time for further studies of the same kind.

A book that meets all the conditions stated is 1 Thessalonians, written by the apostle Paul. It is quite short, it does not have much difficulty of interpretation, meaning, or doctrine, and it is exceedingly rich in its teaching. It has the further advantage of being the first in time of Paul's epistles. Another book to consider is 1 John, which is not a difficult book in most respects, and it is one of the richest books in the Bible.

The second work to do is to master the general contents of the book.

The way to do this is very simple. It consists in merely reading the book through, without stopping, and then reading it through again, and then again, maybe a dozen times in all, at a single sitting. To someone who has never tried it, it does not seem as if that would amount to much, but any thoughtful person who has ever tried it will tell you quite differently. It is simply wonderful how a book takes on new meaning and beauty upon this sort of an acquaintance. It begins to open up. New relations between different parts of the book begin to reveal themselves. Fascinating lines of thought running through the book appear. The book is grasped as a whole. The relation of the various parts to one another is recognized, and a foundation is laid for an intelligent study of those parts in detail.

James M. Gray of Boston, a great lover of the Bible and prominent teacher of it, says that for many years of his ministry he had an inadequate and unsatisfactory knowledge of the English Bible. The first practical idea that he received in the study of the English Bible was from a layman. The brother possessed an unusual serenity and joy in his Christian experience, which he attributed to his reading of Paul's letter to the Ephesians.

Mr. Gray asked him how he had read it, and he said he had taken a pocket copy of Ephesians into the woods one Sunday afternoon and had read it through at a single sitting. He said that he had read it through as many as a dozen times before stopping, and by the time he had left the woods, he had gotten possession of Ephesians, or rather, its wondrous truths had gotten possession of him. This was the secret, simple as it was, for which Mr. Gray had been waiting and praying. From this time on, Mr. Gray studied his Bible through in this way, and it became a new book to him.

The third work is to prepare an introduction to the book.

Write down at the top of separate sheets of paper or cards the following questions:

- Who wrote this book?

- To whom did he write?

- Where did he write it?

- When did he write it?

- What was the occasion of his writing?

- What was the purpose for which he wrote?

- What were the circumstances of the author when he wrote?

- What were the circumstances of those to whom he wrote?

- What glimpses does the book give into the life and character of the author?

- What are the main ideas of the book?

- What is the central truth of the book?

- What are the characteristics of the book?

Having prepared your sheets of paper with these questions at the top, lay them side by side on your study table before you. Go through the book slowly, and as you come to an answer to any of these questions, write it down on the appropriate sheet of paper. It may be necessary to go through the book several times to do the work thoroughly and satisfactorily, but you will be amply repaid. When you have finished your own work in this way, and not until then, it would be good, if possible, to compare your results with those reached by others. A book that will serve as a good illustration of this introductory work is *The New Testament and Its Writers*, by James Alexander McClymont.

The introduction you prepare for yourself will be worth many times more to you than any that you can obtain from others. The work itself is a rare education in the ability to perceive, compare, and reason.

The answers to our questions will sometimes be found in some related book. For example, if we are studying one of the Pauline Epistles, the answer to our questions may be found in the Acts of the Apostles, or in the epistle written to the place from which the one studied was written. Of course, all the questions given will not apply to every book in the Bible.

If one is not willing to give the time and labor necessary, this introductory work can be omitted, but only at a great cost. Single passages in an epistle can never be correctly understood unless we know to whom they were written. Much false interpretation of the Bible arises from taking some direction clearly intended for local application to be of universal authority. So also, oftentimes false interpretations arise from applying to the unbeliever what was intended for the saint.

Noting the occasion of writing can clear up the meaning of a passage that otherwise would not be understood. Bearing in mind the circumstances of the author when he wrote will frequently give new force to his words. Consider the jubilant epistle to the Philippians, with its often repeated *rejoice in the Lord* and its *Be anxious for nothing, but in everything by prayer and supplication with thanksgiving let your requests be made known to God. And the peace of God, which surpasses all comprehension, will guard your hearts and your minds in Christ Jesus* (Philippians 4:6-7). When you realize that it was written by a prisoner awaiting a possible death sentence, it becomes much more meaningful. Keeping in mind the main purpose for which a book was written will help you better understand the other points and exhortations and how they are all related. In fact, the answers to all the questions will be valuable in all the work that follows, as well as valuable in themselves.

The fourth work is to divide the book into its proper sections.

This work is not absolutely necessary, but it is still

valuable. Go through the book and notice the main divisions in the thought, and mark these. Then go through these divisions and see if there are any natural subdivisions, and mark these. Having discovered the divisions of the book, give to each section an appropriate heading or description. Make this as precise a statement of the general contents of the section as possible. Make it also as short and striking as possible, so that it will attach itself in the mind. As far as possible, let these headings or captions of the subdivisions connect themselves with the general heading of the division. Do not attempt too elaborate a division at first.

The following division of 1 Peter, without many marked subdivisions, will serve as a simple illustration of what is meant:

1. **First Peter 1:1-2.** Introduction and salutation to the pilgrims and sojourners in Pontus, etc.

2. **First Peter 1:3-12.** The inheritance reserved in heaven and the salvation ready to be revealed for those pilgrims who, in the midst of various temptations, are kept by the power of God through faith.

3. **First Peter 1:13-25.** The pilgrim's conduct during the days of his pilgrimage.

4. **First Peter 2:1-10.** The high calling, position, and destiny of the pilgrim people.

5. **First Peter 2:11-12.** The pilgrim's conduct during the days of his pilgrimage.

6. **First Peter 2:13-17.** The pilgrim's duty toward the human governments under which he lives.

7. **First Peter 2:18-3:7.** The duty of various classes of pilgrims.

   a. **First Peter 2:18-25.** The duty of servants toward their masters – enforced by an appeal to Christ's conduct under injustice and reviling.

   b. **First Peter 3:1-6.** The duty of wives toward husbands.

   c. **First Peter 3:7.** The duty of husbands toward their wives.

8. **First Peter 3:8-12.** The conduct of pilgrims toward one another.

9. **First Peter 3:13-22.** The pilgrim suffering for righteousness' sake.

10. **First Peter 4:1-6.** The pilgrim's separation from the practices of those among whom he spends the days of his pilgrimage.

11. **First Peter 4:7-11.** The pilgrim's sojourning drawing to a close and his conduct during the last days.

12. **First Peter 4:12-19.** The pilgrim suffering for and with Christ.

13. **First Peter 5:1-4.** The duty and reward of elders.

14. **First Peter 5:5-11.** The pilgrim's walk – humble

and trustful, watchful and steadfast – and a doxology.

15. First Peter 5:12-14. Conclusion and benediction.

The fifth work is to take up each verse in order and study it.

The first thing to be done in this verse-by-verse study of the book is to get the exact meaning of the verse. How is this to be done?

There are three steps that lead into the meaning of a verse.

The first step is to get the exact meaning of the words used. There will be found two classes of words: (1) those whose meaning is perfectly apparent, and (2) those whose meaning is doubtful. It is quite possible to find the precise meaning of these doubtful words. This is not done by consulting a dictionary. That is an easy, but dangerous, method of finding the scriptural significance of a word.

The only safe and sure method is to study the usage of the word in the Bible itself, and especially of that particular Bible writer of whose writings we are studying. To study the Bible usage of words, one must have a concordance [or utilize Bible study software]. Altogether, the best concordance is *Strong's Exhaustive Concordance of the Bible*. The next best is *Young's Analytical Concordance to the Bible. Cruden's Complete Concordance* will do, if one cannot afford Strong's or Young's.

All the passages in which the word whose meaning is being sought occurs should be found and examined, and in this way the precise meaning of the word will be determined. Many important Bible doctrines depend upon the meaning of a word.

For example, two schools of theology differ on the meaning of the word "justify." The critical question is, does the word "justify" mean "to make righteous," or does it mean "to count or declare righteous"? The correct interpretation of many passages of Scripture turns upon the sense that we give to this word. If you look up all the passages in the Bible in which the word is found, there will be no doubt as to the Bible usage and meaning of the word. Passages such as Deuteronomy 25:1, Exodus 23:7, Isaiah 5:23, Luke 26:15, Romans 2:13 and 3:23-24, Luke 18:14, and Romans 4:2-8 will serve to illustrate the biblical usage.

By the use of Strong's or Young's concordance, the student will see that the same word can be used in the English version to translate several different Greek or Hebrew words. Of course, in determining the biblical usage, we should give special weight to those passages in which the specific English word examined is the translation of the same word in Greek or Hebrew. Either of the concordances mentioned will enable us to do this, even if we are not at all acquainted with Greek or Hebrew. It will be much easier to do it with Strong's concordance than with Young's, though.

It is surprising how many difficult problems in the interpretation of Scripture are solved by the simple examination of the biblical usage of words. For example, one of the burning questions of today is the meaning of 1 John 1:7. Does this verse teach that *the blood of Jesus His Son cleanses us* from all the guilt of sin, or does it teach us that *the blood of Jesus His Son cleanses us* from the very presence of sin, so that by the blood of Christ, indwelling sin is itself eradicated?

Many of those who read this question will answer it offhandedly at once, one way or the other. But the offhanded way of answering questions of this kind is a very bad way. Take your concordance and look up every passage in the Bible in which the word "cleanse" is used in connection with blood, and the question will be answered conclusively and forever. Never conclude that you have the right meaning of a verse until you have carefully determined the meaning of all doubtful words in it by an examination of Bible usage. Even when you are pretty sure you know the meaning of the words, it is good not to be too sure until you have looked them up.

The second step in learning the meaning of a verse is to carefully notice the context (what goes before and what comes after). Many verses, if they stood alone, might be capable of several interpretations, but when what goes before and what comes after is considered, all the interpretations except one are seen to be impossible. For example. look at John 14:18: *I will not leave you as orphans; I will come to you.*

To what does Jesus refer when He says, *I will come to you*? One commentator says that He refers to His reappearance to His disciples after His resurrection to comfort them. Another commentator says that Jesus is referring to His second coming, as it is called. Another one says He refers to His coming through the Holy Spirit's work to make Himself known to His disciples and to make His abode with them. Which does He mean?

When scholars disagree, can an ordinary Christian decide? Very often, yes. Certainly they can in this case. If anyone will carefully note what Jesus is talking about in the verses immediately preceding (verses 15-17) and in the verses immediately following (verses 19-26), he will have no doubt as to what coming Jesus refers to in this passage. You can see this by trying it for yourself.

A very large percentage of the difficult questions of biblical interpretation can be resolved by this very simple method of noticing what goes before and what comes after. Many of the sermons we hear become very absurd when we take the trouble to notice the setting of the preacher's text and how utterly foreign the thought of the sermon is to the thought of the text when regarded in the light of the context.

The third step in determining the correct and precise meaning of a verse is the examination of parallel passages; that is, we can look at passages that treat the same subject – passages, for example, that give another account of the same message or event, or passages that are evidently intended as a commentary on the passage in hand. Very often, after having carefully studied the words used and the context, we will still be in doubt as to which of two or three possible interpretations of a verse is the one intended by the writer or speaker. In such a case, there is always a passage somewhere else in the Bible that will settle this question.

Take for example John 14:3: *I will come again and receive you to Myself, that where I am, there you may be also.* A careful consideration of the words used in their relation to one another will go far in determining the meaning of this passage, but still we find four different interpretations among some worthwhile commentators.

First, the coming referred to here is Christ's coming at death to receive the believer unto Himself, as in the case of Stephen (Acts 7:54-60). Second would be Jesus' coming again at the resurrection. The third interpretation is the coming again through the Holy Spirit. The fourth is the coming again of Christ when He returns personally and gloriously at the end of the age.

Which of these four interpretations is the correct one? What has already been said about verse 18 might seem to settle the question, but it does not, for it is not at all clear that the coming referred to in verse 3 is the same one as in verse 18, for what is said in connection with the two comings is altogether different. In the one case, it is a coming of Christ to *receive you to Myself, that where I am, there you may be also.* In the other case, it is a coming of Christ to make Himself known unto us and to make His abode with us.

Fortunately, there is a verse that settles the question – an inspired commentary on the words of Jesus. This is found in 1 Thessalonians 4:16-17. This will be seen clearly if we arrange the two passages in parallel columns.

John 14:3	1 Thessalonians 4:16-17
I will come again	The Lord Himself will descend.
and receive you to Myself,	We . . . will be caught up . . . to meet the Lord.
that where I am, there you may be also.	So we shall always be with the Lord.

The two passages clearly match exactly in the three facts stated, and beyond a doubt refer to the same event. But if anyone will look at all closely at 1 Thessalonians 4:16-17, there can be no doubt as to what coming of our Lord is referred to there.

The Treasury of Scripture Knowledge[1] will be of great assistance in finding parallel passages. These are the three steps that lead us into the meaning of a verse. They require work, but it is work that anyone can do, and when the meaning of a verse is thus settled, we arrive at conclusions that are correct and fixed. After taking these steps, it is good to consult commentaries and see how our conclusions agree with those of others.

Before we proceed to the next thing to be done with a verse after its meaning has been determined, let it be said that God intended to convey some definite truth in each verse of Scripture, and any interpretation of from two to a dozen interpretations of a verse is not as good as another. With every verse of Scripture, we should not ask what it can be made to teach, but what it was intended to teach – and we should not rest satisfied until we have settled that. Of course, it is admitted that a verse may have a primary meaning and other

1   *The Treasury of Scripture Knowledge* is a book by R. A. Torrey that is a combination of a concordance, a topical Bible, and cross-references.

more remote meanings. For example, a prophecy may have its primary fulfilment in some person or event near at hand, such as Solomon, and a more remote and complete fulfilment in Christ.

After we have determined the meaning of a verse, the next thing to do is to analyze the verse. This is most interesting and profitable work. It is also a rare education of the various capabilities of the intellect.

The way to do it is this: Look steadfastly at the verse and ask yourself, What does this verse teach? Then begin to write down: This verse teaches this, then this, etc. At first glance, you will very likely see only one or two things the verse teaches, but as you look again and again, the teachings will begin to multiply, you will wonder how one verse could teach so much, and you will have an ever-growing sense of the divine authorship of the Bible.

It is related of the younger Professor Agassiz that a young man came to him to study ichthyology. The professor gave him a fish to study and told him to come back when he had mastered that fish and get another lesson. In time, the young man came back and told Professor Agassiz what he had observed about the fish. When he had finished, to his surprise he was given the same fish again and was told to study it further. He came back again, having observed new facts and, as he supposed, all the facts about the fish. But again he was given the same fish to study, and so it went on, lesson after lesson, until that student had been taught what his perceptive powers were for, and also had been taught to do thorough work.

That is the same way that we ought to study the Bible. We ought to come back to the same verse of the Bible again and again, until we have gotten, as far as it is possible to us, all that is in the verse. Then the probability is that when we come back to the same verse several months later, we will find something we did not see before.

It may be that an illustration of this method of analysis will be helpful. Let us take 1 Peter 1:1-2. (Here we have an instance in which the verse division is so clearly illogical and absurd that in our analysis we cannot follow it, but must take the two verses together. This will often be the case.)

Peter, an apostle of Jesus Christ, to those who reside as aliens, scattered throughout Pontus, Galatia, Cappadocia, Asia, and Bithynia, who are chosen according to the foreknowledge of God the Father, by the sanctifying work of the Spirit, to obey Jesus Christ and be sprinkled with His blood: May grace and peace be yours in the fullest measure. (1 Peter 1:1-2)

These verses teach:

1. This epistle is by Peter.

2. The Peter who wrote this epistle was an apostle of Jesus Christ.

3. Peter delighted to think and speak of himself as one sent of Jesus Christ. Compare 2 Peter 1:1. (Note – "apostle" is Greek for Latin "missionary.")

4. The name, Jesus Christ (used twice in these two verses). Significance:

   a. Savior.

   b. Anointed One.

   c. Fulfiller of the Messianic predictions of the Old Testament. "Christ" has reference especially to the earthly reign of Christ.

5. This epistle was written to the elect, especially to the elect who are sojourners of the dispersion in Pontus, Paul's old field of labor. (Note: The question whether speaking of the dispersion implies that the destination of this epistle was to Jewish Christians will have been taken up and answered in the introduction to the epistle.)

6. Believers are:

   a. elect or chosen of God.

   b. foreknown of God.

   c. sanctified of the Spirit.

   d. sprinkled by the blood of Jesus Christ.

   e. sojourners or pilgrims on earth.

   f. subjects of multiplied grace.

   g. possessors of multiplied peace.

7. Election.

   a. Who are the elect? Believers. Compare verse 5.

   b. To what are they elect?

    1. obedience.

    2. sprinkling of the blood of Jesus.

  c. According to what are they elect? The fore-knowledge of God. Compare Romans 8:29-30.

  d. In what are they elect? Sanctification of the Spirit.

  e. The test of election: Obedience. Compare 2 Peter 1:10.

  f. The work of the three persons of the Trinity in election:

    1. The Father foreknows.

    2. Jesus Christ cleanses from guilt by His blood.

    3. The Spirit sanctifies.

8. God is the Father of the elect.

9. The humanity of Christ: seen in the mention of His blood.

10. The reality of the body of Jesus Christ: seen in the mention of His blood.

11. It is by His blood and not by His example that Jesus Christ delivers from sin.

12. Peter's first and great wish and prayer for those to whom he wrote was that grace and peace might be multiplied.

13. It is not enough to have grace and peace. One should have multiplied grace and peace.

14. Simply because people might already have grace and peace is no reason to stop praying for them, but rather is an incentive to pray that they may have more grace and peace.

15. Grace precedes peace. Compare all passages where these words are found together.

This is simply an illustration of what is meant by analyzing a verse. The whole book should be gone through in this way.

There are three rules to be observed in this analytical work.

1. Do not put anything into your analysis that is not clearly in the verse. One of the greatest faults in Bible study is reading into passages what God never put into them. Some people have their pet doctrines and see them everywhere, even where God does not see them. No matter how true, precious, or scriptural a doctrine is, do not put it into your analysis where it is not in the verse. Considerable experience with classes in this kind of study leads me to emphasize this rule.

2. Find all that is in the verse. This rule can only be carried out relatively. Much will escape you because the verses of the Bible contain such wealth, but do not rest until you have dug and dug and dug, and there seems to be nothing more to find.

3. State what you do find just as accurately and exactly as possible. Do not be content with putting into your analysis something close to what is in the verse, but state in your analysis precisely what is in the verse.

The sixth work in the study of the book is to arrange the results obtained by the verse-by-verse analysis.

By your verse-by-verse analysis, you have discovered and recorded a great number of facts. The work now is to get these facts into an orderly shape. To do this, go carefully through your analysis and note the topics discussed in the epistle. Write these topics down as soon as you see them. Having made a complete list of the topics dealt with in the book, write these topics on separate cards or sheets of paper. Then, going through the analysis again, copy each point in the analysis upon its appropriate sheet of paper. For example, copy every point regarding God the Father on the card that has this topic listed at the top.

This general classification should be followed by a more thorough and detailed subdivision. Suppose that we are studying 1 Peter. Having completed our analysis of the epistle and having gone over it carefully, we will find that the following subjects, at least, are mentioned in the epistle:

1. God

2. Jesus Christ

3. The Holy Spirit

4. The Believer

5. Wives and Husbands

6. Servants

7. The New Birth

8. The Word of God

9. Old Testament Scripture

10. The Prophets

11. Prayer

12. Angels

13. The Devil

14. Baptism

15. The Gospel

16. Salvation

17. The World

18. Gospel Preachers and Teachers

19. Heaven

20. Humility

21. Love

These will serve for general headings, but after the material found in the analysis is arranged under these headings, it will subdivide itself naturally into numerous subdivisions.

For example, the material under the heading "God" can be subdivided into these subdivisions:

1. His names. (The material under this heading is quite rich.)

2. His Attributes (This should be subdivided again.):

    a. His Holiness

    b. His Power

    c. His Foreknowledge

    d. His Faithfulness

    e. His Long-suffering

    f. His Grace. There are twenty-five or more points on God's grace in the epistle.

    g. His Mercy

    h. His Impartiality

    i. His Severity

3. God's Judgments

4. God's Will

5. What Is Acceptable to God

6. What Is Due to God

7. God's Dwelling Place

8. God's Dominion

9. God's Work. What God Does.

10. The Things of God

a. The Mighty Hand of God

b. The House of God

c. The Gospel of God

d. The Flock of God

e. The People of God

f. The Bondservants of God

g. The Word of God

h. The Oracles of God, etc.

An illustration in full of the classified arrangement of the teaching of a book on one doctrine will probably show better how to do this work that any abstract statement, and it will also illustrate in part how fruitful this method of study is. We will look at 1 Peter again, this time specifically at its teaching regarding the believer.

What the Epistle Teaches about the Believer

1. The Believer's Privileges

    a. His Election

        1. He is foreknown of the Father, 1:2.

        2. He is elect or chosen of God, 1:1.

        3. He is chosen of God, according to His foreknowledge, 1:2.

        4. He is chosen unto obedience, 1:2.

        5. He is chosen unto the sprinkling of the blood of Jesus, 1:2.

6. He is chosen in sanctification of the Spirit, 1:2.

b. His Calling

  1. By whom called:

    a. God, 1:15.

    b. The God of all grace, 5:10.

  2. To what called:

    a. The imitation of Christ in the patient taking of suffering for well doing, 2:20- 21.

    b. To render blessings for reviling, 3:9.

    c. Out of darkness into God's marvelous light, 2:9.

    d. To God's eternal glory, 5:10.

  3. In whom called:

    a. In Christ, 5:10.

  4. The purpose of his calling:

    a. That he may show forth the praises of Him who called, 2:9.

    b. That he may inherit a blessing, 3:9.

c. His Regeneration

  1. He has been begotten again:

    a. Of God, 1:3.

    b. Unto a living hope, 1:3.

    c. Unto an inheritance imperishable, undefiled, that fades not away, reserved in heaven, 1:4.

    d. By the resurrection of Jesus Christ, 1:3.

    e. Of imperishable seed by the word of God that lives, etc., 1:23.

d. His Redemption

  1. He has been redeemed:

    a. Not with corruptible things, as silver and gold, 1:18.

    b. With precious blood, even the blood of Christ, 1:19.

    c. From his vain manner of life, handed down from his fathers, 1:18.

    d. His sins have been borne by Christ, in His own body, on the tree, 2:24.

e. His Sanctification

  1. He is sanctified by the Spirit, 1:2.

f. His Cleansing

  1. He is cleansed by the blood, 1:2.

g. His Security

  1. He is guarded by the power of God, 1:5.

2. He is guarded unto a salvation ready, or prepared, to be revealed in the last time, 1:5.

3. God cares for him, 5:7.

4. He can cast all his anxiety upon God, 5:7.

5. The God of all grace will perfect, establish, and strengthen him, after a brief trial of suffering, 5:10.

6. None can harm him if he is zealous of that which is good, 3:13.

7. He will not be put to shame, 2:6.

h. His Joy

   1. The character of his joy.

      a. His present joy:

         1. A great joy, 1:8.

         2. An unspeakable joy, 1:8.

         3. A joy full of glory, 1:8.

         4. (Note: This present joy cannot be hindered by being put to grief because of manifold temptations, 1:6.)

      b. His future joy:

         1. Exceeding, 4:13.

   2. In what he rejoices:

      a. In the salvation prepared to be revealed in the last time, 1:6.

      b. Because of his faith in the unseen Jesus Christ, 1:8.

      c. In fellowship in Christ's sufferings, 4:13.

   3. In what he will rejoice:

      a. In the revelation of Christ's glory, 4:13.

      b. (Note: Present joy in fellowship with the sufferings of Christ is the condition of exceeding joy at the revelation of Christ's glory, 4:13).

i. His Hope

   1. Its character:

      a. A living hope, 1:3.

      b. A reasonable hope, 3:15.

      c. An inward hope, *in you*, 3:15.

   2. In whom is his hope:

      a. In God, 1:21.

   3. The foundation of his hope:

      a. The resurrection of Jesus Christ, 1:13-21.

j. His Salvation

   1. A past salvation:

      a. Has been redeemed, 1:18-19.

     b. Has been healed, 2:24.

     c. (Note: By baptism, after a true likeness, the believer, as Noah by the flood, has passed out of the old life of nature into the new resurrection life of grace, 3:21.)

  2. A present salvation:

     a. He is now receiving the salvation of his soul, 1:9.

  3. A growing salvation, through feeding on His word, 2:2.

  4. A future salvation, ready or prepared to be revealed in the last time, 1:5.

k. The Believer's Possessions

  1. God as his Father, 1:17.

  2. Christ as his:

     a. Sin bearer, 2:24.

     b. Example, 2:21.

     c. Fellow sufferer, 4:3.

  3. A living hope, 1:3.

  4. An imperishable, undefiled, unfading inheritance reserved in heaven, 1:4.

  5. Multiplied grace and peace, 1:2.

  6. Spiritual milk without guile for his food, 2:2.

7. Gifts for service – each believer has, or may have, some gift, 4:10.

l. What Believers Are:

1. An elect race, 2:9.

2. A royal priesthood, 2:9

3. A holy priesthood, 2:5.

4. A holy nation, 2:9.

5. A people for God's own possession, 2:9.

6. Living stones, 2:5.

7. The house of God, 4:17.

8. A spiritual house, 2:5.

9. The flock of God, 5:2.

10. Children of obedience, 1:14.

11. Partakers of, or partners in, Christ's sufferings, 4:13.

12. Partakers of, or partners in, the glory to be revealed, 5:1.

13. Sojourners or strangers, 1:1.

14. Foreigners on earth: he has no civil rights here; his citizenship is in heaven, 2:11. Compare Philippians 3:20.

15. A sojourner on his way to another country, 2:1.

16. A Christian: representative of Christ, 4:16.

m. The Believer's Possibilities

    1. He may die unto sin, 2:24.

    2. He may live unto righteousness, 2:24.

    3. (Note: We must die unto sin if we are to live unto righteousness, 2:24.)

    4. He may follow in Christ's steps, 2:21.

    5. He may cease from sin, 4:1.

    6. He may cease from living to the lusts of men, 4:2.

    7. He may live unto the will of God, 4:2.

    8. (Note: It is through suffering in the flesh that he ceases from sin and living to the lusts of men, and lives to the will of God.)

n. What Was for the Believer

    1. The ministry of the prophets was in his behalf, 1:12.

    2. The preciousness of Jesus is for him, 2:7.

o. Unclassified

    1. Has the gospel preached to him in the Holy Spirit, 1:12.

    2. Grace is to be brought unto him at the revelation of Jesus Christ, 1:3. Compare Ephesians 3:7.

    3. Has tasted that the Lord is gracious, 2:3.

2. The Believer's Trial and Sufferings

   a. The fact of the believer's sufferings and trials, 1:6.

   b. The nature of the believer's sufferings and trials:

      1. He endures griefs, suffering wrongfully, 2:19.

      2. He suffers for righteousness' sake, 3:14.

      3. He suffers for well doing, 2:20; 3:17.

      4. He suffers as a Christian, 4:16.

      5. He is subjected to manifold temptations, 1:6.

      6. He is put to grief in manifold temptations, 1:6.

      7. He is spoken against as an evil doer, 2:12.

      8. His good manner of life is reviled, 3:16.

      9. He is spoken evil of because of his separated life, 4:4.

      10. He is reproached for the name of Christ, 4:14.

      11. He is subjected to fiery trials, 4:12.

   c. Encouragements for believers undergoing fiery trials and suffering.

      1. It is better to suffer for well doing than for evil doing, 3:17.

2. Judgment must begin at the house of God, and the present judgment of believers through trial is not comparable to the future end of those who obey not the gospel, 4:17.

3. Blessed is the believer who suffers for righteousness' sake, 3:14. Compare Matthew 5:10-12.

4. Blessed is the believer who is reproached for the name of Christ, 4:14.

5. The Spirit of glory and the Spirit of God rests upon the believer who is reproached for the name of Christ, 4:14.

6. The believer's grief is for a little while, 1:6.

7. The believer's suffering is for a little while, 5:10.

8. Suffering for a little while will be followed by God's glory in Christ, which is eternal, 5:10.

9. The suffering endured for a little while is for the testing of faith, 1:7.

10. The fiery trial is for a test, 4:12.

11. The faith thus proved is more precious than gold, 1:7.

12. Faith proven by manifold temptations will be found unto praise, honor, and glory at the revelation of Jesus Christ, 1:7.

13. It is that his proved faith may be found unto praise and glory and honor at the revelation of Jesus Christ that the believer is for a little while subjected to manifold temptations, 1:7.

14. It is pleasing to God when a believer, for conscience toward God, endures grief, suffering wrongfully, 2:19.

15. It is pleasing to God when a believer takes it patiently, when he does well and suffers for it, 2:20.

16. Through suffering in the flesh, we cease from sin, 4:1.

17. Those who speak evil of us will give account to God, 4:5.

18. Sufferings are being shared by fellow believers, 5:9.

19. Christ suffered for us, 2:21.

20. Christ suffered for sins once (or once for all), the righteous for the unrighteous, that He might bring us to God, being put to death in the flesh, but made alive in the spirit, 3:18.

21. Christ left the believer an example that he should follow in His steps, 2:21.

22. In our fiery trials we are made partakers of, or partakers in, Christ's sufferings, 4:13.

23. When His glory is revealed, we will be glad also with exceeding joy, 4:13.

d. How the believer should meet his trial and sufferings.

1. The believer should not regard his fiery trial as a strange thing, 4:12.

2. The believer should expect fiery trial, 4:12.

3. When the believer suffers as a Christian, let him not be ashamed, 4:16.

4. When the believer suffers as a Christian, let him glorify God in this name, 4:16.

5. When the believer suffers fiery trials, he should rejoice, insomuch as he is made a partaker of Christ's suffering, 4:13.

6. When the believer suffers, let him not return reviling with reviling, or suffering with threatening, but commit himself to Him who judges righteously, 2:23.

7. When the believer suffers, he should in well doing commit the keeping of his soul unto God, as unto a faithful Creator, 4:19.

3. The Believer's Dangers

a. The believer may fall into fleshly lusts that war against the soul, 2:11.

b. The believer may sin, 2:20.

   c. The believer may fall into sins of the most serious kind, 4:15.

      1. (Notice in this verse the awful possibilities that lie dormant in the heart of at least a sincere professed believer.)

   d. The believer's prayers may be hindered, 3:7.

   e. The believer is in danger that his high calling and destiny might tempt him to despise human laws and authority, 2:13.

   f. The believer is in danger that his high calling might lead him to lose sight of his lowly obligations to human masters, 2:18.

   g. Young believers are in danger of disregarding the will and authority of older believers. 5:15.

4. The Believer's Responsibility

   a. Each believer has an individual responsibility, 4:10.

   b. Each believer's responsibility is for the gift he has received, 4:10.

5. The Believer's Duties

   a. What the believer should be:

      1. Be holy in all manner of living.

         a. Because God is holy, 1:15.

         b. Because it is written, *You shall be holy*, 1:16.

2. Be like Him who called him, 1:15-16.

3. Be sober (or of a calm, collected, thoughtful spirit,), 1:13; 4:7; 5:8.

4. Be sober (or of a calm, etc.) unto prayer, 4:7.

5. Be of a sound mind, because the end of all things is approaching, 4:7.

6. Be watchful, 5:8.

7. Be steadfast in the faith, 5:9.

8. Be subject to every ordinance of man.

    a. For the Lord's sake, 2:13.

    b. To the king, as supreme, 2:13.

    c. To governors, as sent by the king for the punishment of evildoers, and for praise to those who do well, 2:14.

    d. Because this is God's will, 2:15.

9. Be like-minded, 3:8.

10. Be sympathetic, 3:8.

11. Be tenderhearted, 3:8.

12. Be humble-minded, 3:8.

13. Be ready:

    a. Always. 3:15.

    b. To give an answer to every man that asks a reason of the hope that is in him, 3:15.

    c. With gentleness and reverence, 3:15.

    d. In order to put to shame those who revile their good manner of life in Christ, 3:16.

  14. Should not be troubled, 3:14.

b. What the believer should not do:

    1. The believer should not be conformed according to the lusts of the old life of ignorance, 1:14.

    2. The believer should not render evil for evil, 3:9.

    3. The believer should not render insult for insult, 3:9.

    4. The believer should not fear the world's fear, 3:14.

    5. The believer should not live his remaining time in the flesh to the lusts of men, 4:2.

c. What the believer should do:

    1. He should live as a child of obedience, 1:14.

    2. Pass the time of his sojourning here in fear, 1:17.

    3. Abstain from fleshly lusts that war against the soul, 2:11.

    4. Observe God's will as the absolute law of life, 2:15.

5. Let his conscience be governed by the thought of God and not by the conduct of men, 2:19.

6. Sanctify Christ in his heart as Lord, 3:15. Compare Isaiah 8:13.

7. Live his remaining time in the flesh to the will of God, 4:2.

8. Put away:

   a. All malice, 2:1.

   b. All guile, 2:1.

   c. Hypocrisies, 2:1.

   d. Envies, 2:1.

   e. All evil speaking, 2:1.

9. Come unto the Lord as unto a living stone, 2:4.

10. Show forth the excellencies of Him who called him out of darkness into His marvelous light, 2:9.

11. Arm himself with the mind of Christ; i.e. to suffer in the flesh, 4:1.

12. Cast all his care upon God because He cares for him, 5:7.

13. Stand fast in the true grace of God, 5:12.

14. Withstand the devil, 5:9.

15. Humble himself under the mighty hand of God, 5:5:

    a. Because God resists the proud and gives grace unto the humble, 5:5-6.

    b. That God may exalt him in due time, 5:6.

16. Glorify God when he suffers as a Christian, 4:16.

17. See to it that he does not suffer as a thief or as an evil doer or as a meddler in other people's matters, 4:15.

18. Rejoice in fiery trial, 4:12-13.

19. Toward various persons:

    a. Toward God – fear, 2:17.

    b. Toward the king – honor, 2:17.

    c. Toward masters – be in subjection with all fear (not only to the good and gentle, but to the forward), 2:18.

    d. Toward the brotherhood:

       1. Love, 1:22; 2:17; 4:8.

       2. Love from the heart, 1:22.

       3. Love fervently – intensely, 1:22; 4:8.

       4. Gird themselves with humility as with a slave's apron unto one another:

        a. Be one another's slaves.

        b. Wear humility as a token of their readiness to serve one another, 5:5. Compare John 13:4-5.

    5. Minister the gift he has received from God among the brethren as a good steward of the manifold grace of God, 4:10.

    6. Use hospitality one to another without murmuring, 4:9.

    7. Salute one another with a holy kiss, 5:14.

e. Toward his revilers:

    1. Render blessing for reviling, 3:9.

f. Toward the gentiles:

    1. Have his behavior excellent among the gentiles, 2:12.

    2. Notes: The reason why he should have his behavior excellent among the gentiles is so the gentiles might glorify God in the day of visitation, 2:12. This behavior should consist in good works that the gentiles could observe, 2:12.

g. Toward foolish people:

1. By well doing, put to silence their ignorance, 2:15.

h. Toward all people – honor, 2:17.

1. Note: The special duties of believing husbands and wives toward one another comes under a special classification.

20. Long for the sincere milk of the Word, 2:2.

21. Gird up the loins of his mind, 1:13.

22. Grow, 2:2.

23. Set his hope perfectly on the grace to be brought unto him at the revelation of Jesus Christ, 1:13.

6. The Believer's Characteristics

a. His faith and hope are in God, 1:21.

b. Believes in God through Jesus Christ, 1:21.

c. Calls on God as Father, 1:17.

d. Believes in Christ, though he has never seen Him, 1:8.

e. Loves Christ, though he has never seen Him, 1:8.

f. Is returned unto the Shepherd and Bishop of his soul, 2:25.

g. Has purified his soul in obedience to the truth, 1:22.

    h. Has sincere love for the brethren, 1:22.

    i. Has a good manner of life, 3:16.

    j. Does not run with the gentiles among whom he lives to the same excess of riot (lives a separated life), 4:4.

    k. Keeps his tongue from evil, 3:10.

    l. Keeps his lips from speaking deceit, 3:10.

    m. Turns away from evil, 3:11.

    n. Does good, 3:11.

    o. Seeks peace, 3:11.

    p. Pursues peace, 3:11.

7. The Believer's Warfare

    a. The believer has a warfare before him, 4:1.

    b. The mind of Christ is the proper armament for this warfare, 4:1.

    c. The warfare is with the devil, 5:8-9.

    d. Victory is possible for the believer, 5:9.

    e. Victory is won through steadfastness in the faith, 5:9.

We come now to the seventh and last work. This is simply to meditate upon, and so digest, the results obtained.
At first thought it might seem that when we had completed our classification of results that our work was

finished, but this is not so. These results are for use. They are first for our personal enjoyment and use, and then they can be given out to others. The results can be utilized and applied by meditation upon them. We are no more finished with a book after we have carefully and fully classified its contents than we are finished with a meal after we have arranged it in an orderly way upon the table. It is there to be eaten, digested, and absorbed.

One of the great failures in much of the Bible study of the day is right at this point. There is observation, analysis, and classification, but no meditation. There is perhaps nothing as important in Bible study as meditation. (See Joshua 1:8 and Psalm 1:2-3.) Take your arranged notes and go slowly over them, considering them point by point until these wonderful truths live before you, sink into your soul, live in you, and become part of your life. Do this again and again. Nothing will go further than meditation to make one great and fresh and original as a thinker and speaker. Very few people in this world think.

The method of study outlined in this chapter can be shortened to suit the time and work of the student. For example, one can omit the fifth work (to take up each verse in order and study it) and proceed at once to go through the book as a whole, writing down its teachings on different doctrines. This will greatly shorten and lighten the work. It will also greatly detract from the richness of the results, it will not be as thorough, as accurate, or as scholarly, and it will not be nearly so good of a mental discipline. But many people are lazy, and everybody is in a hurry. So if you will not follow the full plan, the shorter is suggested. But anyone can be a scholar, if he wants to be, at least in the most important area – that of biblical study.

An even briefer plan of book study, and yet one that is very profitable (if one has no time for anything better), is to do the second work (master the general contents of the book), and then go through the epistle verse by verse, looking up all the references given in *The Treasury of Scripture Knowledge*. However, I urge every reader to try the full method described in this chapter with at least one short book in the Bible.

Chapter 3

Topical Study

A second method of Bible study is the Topical Method. This consists in searching through the Bible to find out what its teaching is on various topics. It is perhaps the most fascinating method of Bible study. It yields the largest immediate results, though not the largest ultimate results. It has advantages. The only way to master any topic is to go through the Bible and find what it has to teach on that topic. Almost any great subject will take a remarkable hold upon the heart of a Christian if he will take time to go through the Bible, from Genesis to Revelation, and note what it has to say on that topic. He will have a fuller and more correct understanding of that topic than he ever had before.

It is said of Mr. Moody that he took up the study of "grace" in this way many years ago. Day after day he went through the Bible, studying what it had to say about grace. As the Bible doctrine unfolded before his mind, his heart began to burn, until at last, full of the subject and on fire with the subject, he ran out to the street, and taking hold of the first man he met, he said, "Do you know grace?"

"Grace who?" was the reply.

"The grace of God that brings salvation." Then he just poured out his soul on that subject. If any child of God will study "grace," "love," "faith," "prayer," or any other great Bible doctrine in that way, his soul, too, will become full of the topic. Jesus evidently studied the Old Testament in this way, for we read that *beginning with Moses and with all the prophets, He explained to them the things concerning Himself in all the Scriptures* (Luke 24:27). This method of study made the hearts of the two who walked with Him to burn within them (Luke 24:32). Paul seems to have followed his Master in this method of study and teaching (Acts 17:2-3).

But the method has its dangers. Its very fascination is a danger. Many are drawn by the fascination of this method of study to give up all other methods of study, and this is a great misfortune. A well-rounded, thorough-going knowledge of the Bible is not possible by this method of study. No one method of study will do if one desires to be a well-rounded and well-balanced Bible student.

The greatest danger is that everyone is almost certain to have some field of topics in which he is especially interested, and if he studies his Bible topically, unless he is warned, he is more than likely to go over certain topics again and again. He will be very strong in this line of truth, but will neglect other topics of equal importance, thus becoming a one-sided person. We never know one truth correctly until we know it in its proper relations to other truths.

I know of people, for example, who are interested in the great doctrine of the Lord's second coming, and pretty much all their Bible studies are in that area. This certainly is a precious doctrine, but there are other doctrines in the Bible that a person needs to know, and it is foolish to study this doctrine alone. I know others whose entire interest and study seems to center in the subject of divine healing. I was told about one man who confided to a friend that he had devoted his time for years to the study of the number seven in the Bible. This last is doubtless an extreme case, but it illustrates the danger in topical study.

It is certain that we will never master the whole range of Bible truth if we pursue the Topical Method alone. A few rules concerning topical study will probably be helpful to most of the readers of this book.

Be Systematic
Do not follow your whims in the choice of topics. Do not just take up any topic that happens to suggest itself to you. Make a list of all the subjects that you can think of that are dealt with in the Bible. Make it as comprehensive and complete as possible. Then take these topics up one by one in logical order. The following list of topics is given as a suggestion. Each person can add to the list for himself and subdivide the general subjects into proper subdivisions.

List of topics:

God

- God as a Spirit
- The Unity of God
- The Eternity of God
- The Omnipresence of God
- The Personality of God
- The Omnipotence of God
- The Omniscience of God
- The Holiness of God
- The Love of God
- The Righteousness of God
- The Mercy or Loving-kindness of God
- The Faithfulness of God
- The Grace of God

Jesus Christ

- The Divinity of Christ
- The Subordination of Jesus Christ to the Father
- The Human Nature of Jesus Christ
- The Character of Jesus Christ
  - His Holiness

- His Love to God
- His Love to Man
- His Love for Souls
- His Compassion
- His Prayerfulness
- His Meekness and Humility

- The Death of Jesus Christ
  - The Purpose of Christ's Death
  - Why Did Christ die?
  - For Whom Did Christ Die?
  - The Results of Christ's Death

- The Resurrection of Jesus Christ
  - The Fact of the Resurrection
  - The Results of the Resurrection
  - The Importance of the Resurrection
  - The Manner of the Resurrection

- The Ascension and Exaltation of Jesus Christ

- The Return or Coming Again of Jesus Christ
  - The Fact of His Coming Again
  - The Manner of His Coming Again
  - The Purpose of His Coming Again

- ◆ The Results of His Coming Again
- ◆ The Time of His Coming Again
- The Reign of Jesus Christ

The Holy Spirit

- Personality of the Holy Spirit
- Deity of the Holy Spirit
- Distinction of the Holy Spirit from God the Father and the Son, Jesus Christ
- The Subordination of the Holy Spirit to the Father and to the Son
- Names of the Holy Spirit
- The Work of the Holy Spirit:
  - ◆ In the Universe
  - ◆ In Man in General
  - ◆ In the Believer
  - ◆ In the Prophet and Apostle
  - ◆ In Jesus Christ

Man

- His Original Condition
- His Fall
- The Present Standing before God and

Present Condition of Man outside of the Redemption that is in Jesus Christ

- The Future Destiny of those who Reject the Redemption that is in Jesus Christ

- Justification

- The New Birth

- Adoption

- The Believer's Assurance of Salvation

- The Flesh

- Sanctification

- Cleansing

- Consecration

- Faith

- Repentance

- Prayer

- Thanksgiving

- Praise

- Worship

- Love to God

- Love to Jesus Christ

- Love to Man

- The Future Destiny of Believers

Angels

- Their Nature and Position
- Their Number
- Their Abode
- Their Character
- Their Work
- Their Destiny

Satan or the Devil

- His Existence
- His Nature and Position
- His Abode
- His Work
- Our Duty Regarding Him
- His Destiny

Demons

- Their Existence
- Their Nature
- Their Work
- Their Destiny

For a student who has the perseverance to carry it through, it might be recommended to begin with the first topic on a list like this and go right through it to the end, searching for everything the Bible has to say on these topics. This is what I have done, and have thereby gained a fuller knowledge of truth along these lines, and an immeasurably more vital grasp of the truth than I ever obtained by somewhat extended studies in systematic theology.

Many, however, will stagger at the seeming immensity of the undertaking. To these people it is recommended to begin by selecting those topics that seem more important, but sooner or later settle down to a thorough study of what the Bible has to teach about God and man. The "Abstract of Subjects, Doctrinal and Practical," in the back of the *Bible Text Cyclopedia* by James Inglis will be very helpful.

Be Thorough

Whenever you are studying any topic, do not be content with examining only some of the passages in the Bible that bear upon the subject, but find, as much as possible, every passage in the Bible that bears on this subject. As long as there is a single passage in the Bible on any subject that you have not considered, you have not yet gotten a thoroughly true knowledge of that subject.

How can we find all the passages in the Bible that bear on any subject? First, by the use of a concordance. Look up every passage that has the word in it. Then look up every passage that has synonymous words in it. If, for example, you are studying the subject of prayer, look up every passage that has the word "pray" and its derivatives in it, and also every passage that has such words as "cry," "call," "ask," "supplication," "intercession," etc.

Second, by the use of a book of Bible texts, or a topical Bible. These books arrange the passages of Scripture, not by the words used, but by topics, and there are many verses, for example, on prayer, that do not have the word "prayer" or any synonymous word in them. Incomparably the best topical book of biblical texts is Inglis' *Bible Text Cyclopedia*.[2]

Third, passages not discovered by the use of either a concordance or a topical book will come to light as we study by books or as we read the Bible through in order, and so our treatment of topics will be ever broadening.[3]

Be Exact

Get the exact meaning of each passage considered. Study each passage in its connection, and find its meaning in the way suggested in chapter 2 on the study of individual books of the Bible. Topical study is frequently carried on in a very careless manner. Passages, torn from their connection and context, are strung or huddled together because of some superficial connection with one another and without much regard to their real sense and teaching, and some people call this "topical study." This has brought the whole method of topical study into disrepute. But it is possible to be as exact and scholarly in topical study as in any other method, and when we are, the results will be instructive and

2 *Nave's Topical Bible* will also be helpful.

3 Many of these and other books can be found on software programs. One such program is e-Sword (e-sword.net), that can be downloaded for free and has many great free resources.

gratifying rather than misleading. However, if the work is done in a careless, inexact way, then the results are sure to be misleading and unsatisfactory.

Classify and Write Down Your Results

In the study of any large subject, one will gather a great deal of information. Having gotten it, it must now be organized. As you look it over carefully, you will soon see the facts that belong together. Arrange them together in a logical order.

An illustrative topical study is given below regarding what the Bible teaches concerning the deity of Jesus Christ.

Jesus Christ: His Deity

1. **Divine Names**

   a. Luke 22:70. *They all said, "Are You the Son of God, then?" And He said to them, "Yes, I am."* **The Son of God.** This name is given to Christ forty times. Besides this, the synonymous expression "His son," or "My son," are of frequent occurrence. That this name is used of Christ as a distinctly divine name appears from John 5:18: *For this reason therefore the Jews were seeking all the more to kill Him, because He not only was breaking the Sabbath, but also was calling God His own Father, making Himself equal with God.*

   b. John 1:18. *No one has seen God at any time; the only begotten God who is in the bosom of* the Father, He has explained Him. **The only begotten Son.** This occurs five times. It is evident that the statement that Jesus Christ is the Son of God only in the same sense that all men are sons of God, is not true. Compare Mark 12:6: *He had one more to send, a beloved son; he sent him last of all to them, saying, "They will respect my son."* Here Jesus Himself, having spoken of all the prophets as servants of God, speaks of Himself as *one* and *a beloved son.*

c. Revelation 1:17. *When I saw Him, I fell at His feet like a dead man. And He placed His right hand on me, saying, "Do not be afraid; I am the first and the last."* **The first and the last.** Compare Isaiah 41:4; 44:6. In these latter passages it is the Lord God who is the first and the last.

d. Revelation 22:12-13, 16. *Behold, I am coming quickly, and My reward is with Me, to render to every man according to what he has done. I am the Alpha and the Omega, the first and the last, the beginning and the end. . . . I, Jesus, have sent My angel to testify to you these things for the churches. I am the root and the descendant of David, the bright morning star.* First, **the Alpha and the Omega**. Second, **the beginning and the end**. In Revelation 1:8, it is the Lord God who is the Alpha and the Omega.

e. Acts 3:14. *You disowned the Holy and Righteous One and asked for a murderer to be granted to you.* **The Holy One.** In Hosea 11:9 and many other passages, it is God who is the Holy One.

f. Malachi 3:1: Luke 2:11; Acts 9:17; John 20:28; Hebrews 1:11. *Today in the city of David there has been born for you a Savior, who is Christ the Lord* (Luke 2:11). **The Lord.** This name or title is used of Jesus several hundred times. The word translated "Lord" is used in the New Testament in speaking of men a few times, but not at all in the way in which it is used of Christ. He is spoken of as "the Lord" just as God is. Compare Acts 4:26 with Acts 4:33. Note also Matthew 22:43-45, Philippians 2:11, and Ephesians 4:5. If anyone doubts the attitude of the apostles of Jesus toward Him as divine, they would do well to read one after another the passages that speak of Him as Lord.

g. Acts 10:36. *The word which He sent to the sons of Israel, preaching peace through Jesus Christ (He is Lord of all).* **Lord of all.**

h. 1 Corinthians 2:8. *The wisdom which none of the rulers of this age has understood; for if they had understood it they would not have crucified the Lord of glory.* **The Lord of Glory.** In Psalm 24:8-10, it is *the LORD of hosts* who is *the King of glory.*

   i. Isaiah 9:6. *For a child will be born to us, a son will be given to us; and the government will rest on His shoulders; and His name will be called Wonderful Counselor, Mighty God, Eternal Father, Prince of Peace.*

      1. Wonderful (Compare Judges 13:18.)

      2. Mighty God

      3. Eternal Father

   j. Hebrews 1:8. *Of the Son He says, "Your throne, O God, is forever and ever, And the righteous scepter is the scepter of His kingdom."* **God.** In John 20:28, Thomas calls Jesus *my God*, and is gently rebuked for not believing it before.

   k. Matthew 1:23. *"Behold, the virgin shall be with child and shall bear a Son, and they shall call His name Immanuel," which translated means, "God with us."* **God with us.**

   l. Titus 2:13. *Looking for the blessed hope and the appearing of the glory of our great God and Savior, Christ Jesus.* **Our great God.**

   m. Romans 9:5. *Whose are the fathers, and from whom is the Christ according to the flesh, who is over all, God blessed forever. Amen.* **God blessed forever.**

Proposition: Sixteen names clearly implying Deity are used of Christ in the Bible, some of them over and over again, the total number of passages reaching far into the hundreds.

2. Divine Attributes

   a. Omnipotence

      1. Luke 4:39. *He rebuked the fever, and it left her.* **Jesus has power over disease**; it is subject to His word.

      2. Luke 7:14-15; 8:54-55; John 5:25. *He said, "Young man, I say to you, arise!" The dead man sat up and began to speak* (Luke 7:14-15). **The Son of God has power over death**; it is subject to His word.

      3. Matthew 8:26-27. *He got up and rebuked the winds and the sea, and it became perfectly calm. The men were amazed, and said, "What kind of a man is this, that even the winds and the sea obey Him?"* **Jesus has power over the winds and sea**; they are subject to His word.

      4. Matthew 8:16; Luke 4:35-36, 41. *They brought to Him many who were demon-possessed; and He cast out the spirits with a word, and healed all who were ill* (Matthew 8:16). **Jesus, the Christ, the Son of God, has power over demons**; they are subject to His word.

      5. Ephesians 1:20-23. *Which He brought about in Christ, when He raised Him from the dead and seated Him at His right hand in the heavenly places, far above all rule*

and authority and power and dominion, and every name that is named, not only in this age but also in the one to come. And He put all things in subjection under His feet, and gave Him as head over all things to the church, which is His body, the fullness of Him who fills all in all. **Christ is far above all principality and power and might and dominion** and every name that is named, not only in this world, but also in that which is to come. All things are in subjection under His feet. All the hierarchies of the angelic world are under Him.

6. Hebrews 1:3. *He is the radiance of His glory and the exact representation of His nature, and upholds all things by the word of His power.* **The Son of God upholds all things by the word of His power.**

Proposition: Jesus Christ, the Son of God, is omnipotent.

b. Omniscience

1. John 4:16-19. *He said to her, "Go, call your husband and come here." The woman answered and said, "I have no husband." Jesus said to her, "You have correctly said, 'I have no husband'; for you have had five husbands, and the one whom you now have is not your husband; this you have said truly." The woman said to Him, "Sir, I perceive that You are a prophet."* **Jesus**

knows people's lives, even their secret history.

2. Mark 2:8; Luke 5:22; John 2:24-25; Acts 1:24. *Immediately Jesus, aware in His spirit that they were reasoning that way within themselves, said to them, "Why are you reasoning about these things in your hearts? (Mark 2:8).* **Jesus knows our secret thoughts.** He knows all people. He knows what is in our hearts. (Compare 2 Chronicles 6:30; Jeremiah 17:9-10. Here we see that God alone knows the hearts of the children of men.)

3. John 6:64. *Jesus knew from the beginning who they were who did not believe, and who it was that would betray Him.* Jesus knew from the beginning that Judas would betray Him. Not only does Jesus know our present thoughts, but **He knows our future choices**.

4. John 1:48. *Nathanael said to Him, "How do You know me?" Jesus answered and said to him, "Before Philip called you, when you were under the fig tree, I saw you."* **Jesus knew what people were doing at a distance.**

5. Luke 22:10, 12; John 13:1; Luke 5:4-6. *When He had finished speaking, He said to Simon, "Put out into the deep water*

and let down your nets for a catch." Simon answered and said, "Master, we worked hard all night and caught nothing, but I will do as You say and let down the nets." When they had done this, they enclosed a great quantity of fish, and their nets began to break (Luke 5:4-6). **Jesus knew the future** not only regarding God's acts, but regarding the minute specific acts of people, and even the fishes of the sea.

6. John 16:30; 21:17; Colossians 2:3. *He said to Him, "Lord, You know all things"* (John 21:17). **Jesus knows all things**, and in Him are hid all the treasures of wisdom and knowledge.

Proposition: Jesus Christ is omniscient.

Note: There was, as we shall see when we study the humanity of Christ, a voluntary veiling and renunciation of the exercise of His inherent divine omniscience (Mark 11:12-14; Philippians 2:7).

c. Omnipresence

1. Matthew 18:20. *Where two or three have gathered together in My name, I am there in their midst.* **Jesus Christ is present in every place** where two or three are gathered together in His name.

2. Matthew 28:20. *I am with you always, even to the end of the age.* **Jesus Christ is present**

with everyone who goes forth into any part of the world to make disciples, etc.

3. John 3:13. *No one has ascended into heaven, but He who descended from heaven: the Son of Man.* **The Son of Man was in heaven while He was here on earth.**

4. John 14:20; 2 Corinthians 13:5. *In that day you will know that I am in My Father, and you in Me, and I in you* (John 14:20). **Jesus Christ is in each believer.**

5. Ephesians 1:23. *The fullness of Him who fills all in all.* **Jesus Christ fills all in all.**

Proposition: Jesus Christ is omnipresent.

d. Eternity

1. John 1:1; Micah 5:2; Colossians 1:17; Isaiah 9:6; John 6:62; John 8:58; John 17:5; 1 John 1:1; Hebrews 13:8. *In the beginning was the Word, and the Word was with God, and the Word was God* (John 1:1).

Proposition: The Son of God was from all eternity.

e. Immutability

1. Hebrews 1:12; 13:8. *Jesus Christ is the same yesterday and today and forever* (Hebrews 13:8). **Jesus Christ is unchangeable.** He not only always is, but He always is the same.

2. Philippians 2:6. *Who, although He existed*

in the form of God, did not regard equality with God a thing to be grasped. **Before His incarnation, Jesus Christ was in the form of God.** (Note: *morphe*, translated "form," means "the form by which a person or thing strikes the vision; the external appearance" (From *Thayer's Greek-English Lexicon of the New Testament*).

3. Colossians 2:9. *In Him all the fullness of Deity dwells in bodily form.* **In Christ dwelleth all the fullness of the Godhead in a bodily way.**

Proposition: Five or more distinctively divine attributes are ascribed to Jesus Christ, and all the fullness of the Godhead is said to dwell in Him.

3. Divine Offices

a. Creation

1. Hebrews 1:10; John 1:3; Colossians 1:16. *For by Him all things were created, both in the heavens and on earth, visible and invisible, whether thrones or dominions or rulers or authorities – all things have been created through Him and for Him* (Colossians 1:16). **The Son of God, the eternal Word, the Lord, is creator of all created things.**

b. Preservation

1. Hebrews 1:3. *He is the radiance of His glory*

and the exact representation of His nature, and upholds all things by the word of His power. **The Son of God is the preserver of all things.**

c. The forgiveness of sin

    1. Mark 2:5-10; Luke 7:48-50. *He said to her, "Your sins have been forgiven." Those who were reclining at the table with Him began to say to themselves, "Who is this man who even forgives sins?" And He said to the woman, "Your faith has saved you; go in peace"* (Luke 7:48-50). **Jesus Christ had power on earth to forgive sins.**

    2. Note: Jesus taught that sins were sins against Himself (Luke 7:40-47). Both Simon and the woman as sinners were debtors to Him, but in Psalm 51:4, sin is seen to be against God and God only.

d. Raising of the dead

    1. John 5:28-29; 6:39-44. *Do not marvel at this; for an hour is coming, in which all who are in the tombs will hear His voice, and will come forth; those who did the good deeds to a resurrection of life, those who committed the evil deeds to a resurrection of judgment* (John 5:28-29). **It is Jesus Christ who raises the dead.**

    2. Question: Did not Elijah and Elisha raise

the dead? No; God raised the dead in answer to their prayer, but Jesus Christ will raise the dead by His own word. During the days of His humiliation, it was by prayer that Christ raised the dead. *So they removed the stone. Then Jesus raised His eyes, and said, "Father, I thank You that You have heard Me"* (John 11:41).

e. Transformation of bodies

   1. Philippians 3:21. *[The Lord Jesus Christ] will transform the body of our humble state into conformity with the body of His glory, by the exertion of the power that He has even to subject all things to Himself.* **Jesus Christ will create anew the body of our humiliation into the likeness of His own glorious body.**

f. Judgment

   1. 2 Timothy 4:1. *I solemnly charge you in the presence of God and of Christ Jesus, who is to judge the living and the dead, and by His appearing and His kingdom.* **Christ Jesus will judge the living and the dead.**

   2. Note: Jesus Himself emphasized the divine character of this office. *Not even the Father judges anyone, but He has given all judgment to the Son, so that all will honor the Son even as they honor the Father. He who*

does not honor the Son does not honor the Father who sent Him (John 5:22-23).

g. The bestowal of eternal life

1. John 10:28; 17:2. *I give eternal life to them, and they will never perish; and no one will snatch them out of My hand* (John 10:28). **Jesus Christ is the giver of eternal life.**

Proposition: Seven distinctively divine offices are stated of Jesus Christ.

4. **Statements in the Old Testament that are made specifically about Jehovah God, but in the New Testament refer to Jesus Christ.**

a. Psalm 102:24-27, compare with Hebrews 1:10-12.

b. Isaiah 40:3-4, compare with Matthew 3:3; Luke 1:68-69, 76.

c. Jeremiah 11:20; 17:10, compare with Revelation 2:23.

d. Isaiah 60:19; Zechariah 2:5, compare with Luke 2:32.

e. Isaiah 3:10; 6:1, compare with John 12:37-41.

f. Isaiah 8:13-14, compare with 1 Peter 2:7-8.

g. Isaiah 8:12-13, compare with 1 Peter 3:14-15.

h. Numbers 21:6-7, compare with 1 Corinthians 10:9.

    i.   Psalm 23:1; Isaiah 40:11, compare with John 10:11.

        1. *The LORD is my shepherd, I shall not want* (Psalm 23:1).

        2. *Like a shepherd He will tend His flock, in His arm He will gather the lambs and carry them in His bosom; He will gently lead the nursing ewes* (Isaiah 40:11).

        3. *I am the good shepherd; the good shepherd lays down His life for the sheep* (John 10:11).

    j.   Ezekiel 12:16; 34:11, compare with Luke 19:10.

    k. "LORD" in the Old Testament always refers to God, except when the context clearly indicates otherwise. "Lord" in the New Testament always refers to Jesus Christ, except where the context clearly indicates otherwise.

Proposition: Many statements that refer directly to Jehovah God in the Old Testament refer to Jesus Christ in the New Testament. In New Testament thought and doctrine, Jesus Christ occupies the place that Jehovah occupies in Old Testament thought and doctrine.

  5. The names of God the Father and Jesus Christ the Son are often coupled together.

    a. 2 Corinthians 13:14

        1. *The grace of the Lord Jesus Christ, and the love of God, and the fellowship of the Holy Spirit, be with you all.*

b. Matthew 28:19

c. 1 Thessalonians 3:11

d. 1 Corinthians 12:4-6

e. Titus 3:4-5, compare with Titus 2:13.

f. Romans 1:7. There are many instances of this sort – see all the Pauline Epistles.

g. James 1:1

h. John 14:23, *We* – God the Father and Jesus.

    1. *Jesus answered and said to him, "If anyone loves Me, he will keep My word; and My Father will love him, and We will come to him and make Our abode with him."*

i. 2 Peter 1:1

j. Colossians 2:2

k. John 17:3

l. John 14:1, compare with Jeremiah 17:5-7.

m. Revelation 7:10

n. Revelation 5:13, compare with John 5:23.

Proposition: The name of Jesus Christ is paired with that of God the Father in numerous passages in a way in which it would be impossible to couple the name of any finite being with that of the Deity.

6. Divine worship is to be given to Jesus Christ.

a. Matthew 14:33; 28:9; Luke 24:52, compare with

Matthew 4:9-10; Acts 10:25-26; Revelation 22:8-9.

1. *Behold, Jesus met them and greeted them. And they came up and took hold of His feet and worshiped Him* (Matthew 28:9).

2. *When Peter entered, Cornelius met him, and fell at his feet and worshiped him. But Peter raised him up, saying, "Stand up; I too am just a man"* (Acts 10:25-26).

3. Jesus Christ accepted without hesitation a worship that good men and angels declined with fear (horror).

4. Question: Is not the verb translated "worship" in these passages used of reverence paid to men in high position? Yes, but not in this way by worshippers of Jehovah, as is seen by the way in which Peter and the angel drew back with horror when such worship was offered to them.

b. 1 Corinthians 1:2; 2 Corinthians 12:8-9; Acts 7:59.

1. *To the church of God which is at Corinth, to those who have been sanctified in Christ Jesus, saints by calling, with all who in every place call on the name of our Lord Jesus Christ, their Lord and ours* (1 Corinthians 1:2).

2. Prayer is to be made to Christ.

   c. Psalm 45:11; John 5:23; compare with Revelation 5:8-9, 12-13.

      1. So that all will honor the Son even as they honor the Father. He who does not honor the Son does not honor the Father who sent Him (John 5:23).

      2. It is God the Father's will that all people give the same divine honor to the Son as to Himself.

   d. Hebrews 1:6; Philippians 2:10-11; compare with Isaiah 45:21, 23.

      1. And when He again brings the firstborn into the world, He says, "And let all the angels of God worship Him" (Hebrews 1:6).

      2. The Son of God, Jesus, is to be worshiped as God by people and angels.

Proposition: Jesus Christ is a person to be worshiped by people and angels just as God the Father is worshiped.

General Proposition: God in His Word distinctly proclaims that Jesus Christ is a Divine Being – that He is God. This is shown in all these unmistakable ways:

- By the use of numerous divine names
- By attributing all the distinctively divine attributes to Jesus
- By affirmation of several divine offices
- By referring statements to Jesus Christ in

the New Testament that distinctly name
Jehovah God as their subject in the Old
Testament

- By pairing the name of Jesus Christ together
  with that of God the Father in a way in
  which it would be impossible to couple that
  of any finite being with that of the Deity

- By the clear teaching that Jesus Christ
  should be worshiped even as God the
  Father is worshiped.

One suggestion remains to be made in regard to topical
study: get further topics for topical study from your
book studies.

Chapter 4

Biographical Study

A third method of study is the Biographical. This needs no definition. It consists in taking up the various people mentioned in Scripture and studying their life, work, and character. It is really a special form of topical study. It can be made very interesting and instructive. It is especially useful to the minister for sermon building, but it is also profitable for all Christians.

The following suggestions will help those who are not already experienced in this line of work.

Collect all the passages in the Bible in which the person to be studied is mentioned. This is easily done by turning to the person's name in Strong's concordance, and you will find every passage given in which the person is mentioned.

1. Analyze the character of the person. This will require a repeated reading of the passages in which he is mentioned. This should be done

with pencil in hand so that any characteristic may be written down at once.

2. Note the elements of power and success.

3. Note the elements of weakness and failure.

4. Note the difficulties overcome.

5. Note the helps to success.

6. Note the privileges abused.

7. Note the opportunities neglected.

8. Note the opportunities regarded.

9. Note the mistakes made.

10. Note the perils avoided.

11. Make a sketch of the life in hand. Make it as vivid, living, and realistic as possible. Try to reproduce the subject as a real, living person. Note the place and surroundings of the different events; for example, you could note Paul in Athens, Corinth, Philippi, etc. Note the time relations of the different events. Very few people in reading the Acts of the Apostles, for example, take notice of the rapid passage of time, and so they regard events separated by years as following one another in close sequence. In this connection, note the age or approximate age of the subject at the time of the events recorded of him.

12. Summarize the lessons we should learn from the story of this person's life.

13. Note the person in his relation to Jesus – that is, as a type of Christ (Joseph, David, Solomon, and others), forerunner of Christ, believer in Christ, enemy of Christ, servant of Christ, brother of Christ (James and Jude), friend, etc.

It would be good to begin with someone who does not occupy too much space in the Bible, such as Enoch or Stephen. Of course, many of the points mentioned above cannot be taken up with some characters.

Beneficial books in character studies are James Stalker's *Life of Jesus Christ*, *Life of St. Paul*, and *Imago Christi: The Example of Jesus Christ*; F. B. Meyer's *Elijah and the Secret of His Power*; and also other Old Testament characters, such as those in D. L. Moody's *Bible Characters*.

Chapter 5

Study of Types

A fourth method of study is the Study of Types. We have illustrations of this in the Bible itself, as in the epistle to the Hebrews. It is both an interesting and instructive method of study. It shows us the most precious truths buried away in what once seemed to us a very dry and meaningless portion of the Bible. It hardly needs to be said that this method of study is greatly abused and overdone in some quarters, but that is no reason why we should neglect it altogether, especially when we remember that both Paul and Jesus were fond of this method of study.

The following points may serve as principles to guide us in this method of study:

1. **Be sure you have biblical justification for your supposed type.** If one gives free rein to his imagination in this matter, he can imagine types everywhere, even in places that neither the

human nor divine author of the Book had any intention of a type. Never say that something is a type unless you can point to some clear passage of Scripture where the truth said to be typified is definitely taught.

2. **Begin with the more simple and evident types.** For example, begin with the Passover (compare Exodus 12 with 1 Corinthians 5:7, etc.), the high priest, the tabernacle, etc.

3. **Be on your guard against the imagined and excessive.** Thoughts are almost sure to run wild in anyone who is blessed with any imagination and quickness of typical discernment, unless he holds it in check. Our typical sensitivity and sensibleness will become both quickened and chastened by careful and cautious exercise.

4. **In studying any passage of that you think might possibly be a type, look up all the Scripture references.** The best collection of references is that given in *The Treasury of Scripture Knowledge.*

5. **Carefully study the meaning of the names of people and places mentioned.** Bible names often have very deep and far-reaching meanings. For example, "Hebron," which means "joining together," "union," or "fellowship," is deeply significant when taken in connection with its history, as are all the names of the cities of refuge – and this is true with many Scripture names. Was it accidental that Bethlehem, the

name of the place where the Bread of Life was born, means "house of bread"?

Charles Henry Mackintosh's notes on Genesis, Exodus, Leviticus, Numbers, and Deuteronomy are very good for someone who has had little experience in the study of types.

Chapter 6

Study the Books of
the Bible in Order

A fifth method of Bible study is the old-fashioned method of studying the Bible in order, beginning at Genesis and going right on until Revelation is finished. The Bible can be studied in this way either in the order given in the Bible or in their chronological order.

This method of studying through the Bible in the order given in the Bible is ridiculed much these days, but it has some advantages that no other method of study possesses. It is sometimes said that you might as well begin at the top shelf of your library and read right through as to begin at the beginning of this library of sixty-six books and read right through. A sufficient answer to this is that if you had a library that was important to master as a whole, that you also needed to understand the individual books in it, and that was as well arranged as the Bible is, then this method of going through your library would be excellent.

There are advantages to studying the Bible in order:

First, it is the only method by which you will get an idea of the Book as a whole. The more we know of the Bible as a whole, the better prepared we are for understanding any individual portion of it.

Second, it is the only method by which you are likely to cover the whole Book, and so take in the entire scope of God's revelation. It will be many long years before anyone covers the whole Bible by book studies, or even by topical studies. Every part of God's Word is precious, and there are gems of truth hidden away in most unexpected places. For example, we hit upon some priceless gems in 1 Chronicles 4:10 that we might have missed if we did not study the Bible in order: *Jabez called on the God of Israel, saying, "Oh that You would bless me indeed and enlarge my border, and that Your hand might be with me, and that You would keep me from harm that it may not pain me!" And God granted him what he requested.*

Third, it is the best method to enable one to get hold of the unity of the Bible and its full-of-life character.

Fourth, it is a great corrective to one-sidedness and error. The Bible is a many-sided book: it is Calvinistic and Arminian, it is Trinitarian and Unitarian, it clearly teaches the deity of Christ and insists on His real humanity, it exalts faith and demands works, it urges to victory through conflict and asserts most vigorously that victory is won by faith, etc. If we become too much taken up with any one line of truth in our book or topical studies (and we are more than likely to do so), the daily study of the Bible in order will soon bring us to some contrasting line of truth and bring us back to our proper balance.

Some people become obsessed and become too much occupied with a single line of truth. The thoughtful study of the whole Bible is a great corrective to this tendency. It would be good to have three methods of study in progress at the same time: first, the study of some book; second, the study of topics (perhaps topics suggested by the book studies); and third, the study of the Bible in order.

Every other method of study should be supplemented by studying the Bible in order. Some years ago, I determined to read the King James Version of the Bible through every year, the Revised Version through every year, and the New Testament in Greek through every year. It has proved exceedingly profitable, and I would not willingly give it up.

A sixth method of study is closely related to the fifth method and has advantages of its own that will appear as soon as the method is described. It is studying the various portions of the Bible in their chronological order. In this way the Psalms are read in their historical settings, as are prophecies, epistles, etc.

Chapter 7

Studying the Bible for Practical Usefulness in Dealing with People

The seventh and last method of study is to study the Bible for practical usefulness in dealing with people. To study the Bible in this way, make as complete a classification as possible of all the classes of people that one will meet. Write the names of the different groups at the top of separate sheets of paper or cards. Then begin the Bible and read it through slowly, and when you come to a passage that seems likely to prove useful in dealing with any group, write it down on its appropriate sheet. Go through the entire Bible in this way.

It would be good to have a special Bible for this purpose. You can have different colored pens or highlighters, or different letters or symbols, to represent the different groups – and mark the texts with the applicable color or with the appropriate symbol. The results of the labors of others in this way can be found in a number of books, such as L. W. Munhall's *Furnishing for Workers: A Manual of Scripture Texts for Christian Workers*, Alexander Paterson's *Bible Manual for Christian Workers*, Drury's *Hand-Book for Workers: A Manual of Bible Texts and Readings for Use in Christian Work*, and my *Vest Pocket Companion for Christian Workers* and *How to Bring Men to Christ*.[4] The best book for you, though, is the one you put together yourself. The books mentioned will give you suggestions how to do it.

As a suggestion for beginning in the work, here is a list of classes of people, to which you can add for yourself:

- The careless and indifferent

- Those who wish to be saved but do not know how

- Those who know how to be saved but have difficulties

    - "I am too great a sinner."

    - "My heart is too hard."

    - "I must become better before I become a Christian."

    - "I am afraid I can't hold out."

    - "I am too weak."

    - "I have tried before and failed."

---

4   Torrey's *How to Bring Men to Christ* and many other good books are available through Aneko Press.

- ◆ "I cannot give up my evil ways."

- ◆ "I will be persecuted if I become a Christian."

- ◆ "It will hurt my business."

- ◆ "There is too much to give up."

- ◆ "The Christian life is too hard."

- ◆ "I am afraid of ridicule."

- ◆ "I will lose my friends."

- ◆ "I have no feeling."

- ◆ "I have been seeking Christ, but cannot find Him."

- ◆ "I have sinned away the day of grace."

- ◆ "God won't receive me."

- ◆ "I have committed the unpardonable sin."

- ◆ "It is too late."

- ◆ "Christians are so inconsistent."

- ◆ "God seems to me unjust and cruel."

- ◆ "There are so many things in the Bible that I can't understand."

- ◆ "There is someone I can't forgive."

- Those who are cherishing false hopes

  - ◆ The hope of being saved by a righteous life.

  - ◆ The hope that "God is too good to damn anyone."

- ◆ The hope of being saved by "trying to be a Christian."

- ◆ The hope of being saved, because "I feel saved," or "I feel I am going to heaven."

- ◆ The hope of being saved by a profession of religion, or church membership, or a faith that does not save from sin.

- Those who lack assurance

- Backsliders

- Skeptics

- Infidels

- Those who wish to put off the decision

- Roman Catholics

- Jews

- Spiritualists

- Christian Scientists

- Secret disciples

- The Sorrowing

- The Persecuted

- The Discouraged

- The Despondent

- The Morbid

- Worldly Christians

- The Stingy

The results of this work will be of incalculable value. In the first place, you will get a new view of how perfectly the Bible is adapted to every person's need. In the second place, familiar passages of the Bible will get a new meaning as you see their relation to the needs of people. The Bible will become a very living book to you. In the third place, in seeking food for others, you will be fed yourself. And in the fourth place, you will get a vast amount of material to use in sermons, Bible readings, prayer-meeting talks, and personal work. You will acquire a rare working knowledge of the Bible.

Chapter 8

The Fundamental Conditions of the Most Profitable Bible Study

We have considered seven profitable methods of Bible study. There is something, however, in Bible study more important than the best methods, and that is the fundamental conditions of profitable study. The one who meets these conditions will get more out of the Bible while pursuing the poorest method, than the one who does not meet them will get while pursuing the best method. Many people who are eagerly asking, "What method of Bible study should I pursue?" need something that goes far deeper than a new and better method.

The first of the fundamental conditions of the most profitable Bible study is that the student must be born again. The Bible is a spiritual book. It combines *spiritual thoughts with spiritual words* (1 Corinthians 2:13), and only a spiritual person can understand its deepest and most characteristic and most precious teachings. *A natural man does not accept the things of the Spirit of God, for they are foolishness to him; and he cannot understand them, because they are spiritually appraised* (1 Corinthians 2:14).

Spiritual discernment can be obtained in only one way – by being born again. *Unless one is born again he cannot see the kingdom of God* (John 3:3). No mere knowledge of the human languages in which the Bible was written, however extensive and accurate it may be, will qualify one to understand and appreciate the Bible. One must understand the divine language in which it was written, as well – the language of the Holy Spirit. A person who understands the language of the Holy Spirit, but who does not understand a word of Greek or Hebrew or Aramaic, will get more out of the Bible than one who knows all about Greek and Hebrew and cognate languages, but is not born again, and consequently, does not understand the language of the Holy Spirit.

It is a well-demonstrated fact that many simple men and women who are entirely innocent of any knowledge of the original tongues in which the Bible was written have a knowledge of the real contents of the Bible – its actual teaching – in its depth and fullness and beauty, that surpasses that of many learned professors in theological aptitude. One of the most foolish things of the day is to have unsaved people teach the Bible simply because of their knowledge of the Greek and Hebrew in which the Book was written. It would be just as reasonable to have someone teach art because he had an accurate technical knowledge of paints. It requires aesthetic sense to make someone a competent teacher of art, and it requires spiritual sense to make a man a competent teacher of the Bible.

The person who had aesthetic discernment but little or no technical knowledge of paint would be a far more competent critic of works of art than someone who had much technical knowledge of paint but no aesthetic discernment. In the same way, the man who has no technical knowledge of Greek and Hebrew but who has spiritual discernment is a far more competent critic of the Bible than the one who has much technical knowledge of Greek and Hebrew but no spiritual discernment. It is very unfortunate that in some places more emphasis is placed upon a knowledge of Greek and Hebrew in training for the ministry than is placed upon spiritual life and its consequent spiritual discernment.

Unsaved people should not be forbidden to study the Bible, for the Word of God is the instrument the Holy Spirit uses in the new birth (1 Peter 1:23; James 1:18); but it should be clearly understood that while there are teachings in the Bible that the natural person can understand, and beauties that he can see, its most distinctive and characteristic teachings are beyond his grasp, and its highest beauties belong to a world in which he has no vision.

The first fundamental condition of the most profitable Bible study, then, is that *You must be born again* (John 3:7). You cannot study the Bible to the greatest profit if you have not been born again. Its best treasures are closed to you.

The second condition of the most profitable study is a love for the Bible. A person who eats with an appetite will get far more good out of his meal than someone who eats from a sense of duty. It is good when a student of the Bible can say with Job, *I have treasured the words of His mouth more than my necessary food* (Job 23:12), or with Jeremiah, *Your words were found and I ate them, and Your words became for me a joy and the delight of my heart; for I have been called by Your name, O LORD God of hosts* (Jeremiah 15:16).

Many people come to the table God has spread in His Word with no appetite for spiritual food, and then go here and there grumbling about everything. Spiritual indigestion lies at the root of much modern criticism of the Bible.

How can someone get love for the Bible? First of all, by being born again. Where there is life, there is likely to be appetite. A dead person never hungers. This brings us back to the first condition. But going beyond this, the more vitality there is, the more hunger there is. Abounding life means abounding hunger for the Word. Study of the Word stimulates love for the Word.

I can well remember the time when I had more appetite for books about the Bible than for the Bible itself, but with increasing study there has come increasing love for the Book. Bearing in mind who the author of the Book is, what its purpose is, what its power is, and what the riches of its contents are, will go far toward stimulating a love and appetite for the Book.

The third condition is a willingness to do hard work. Solomon has given a vivid picture of the Bible student who gets the most profit out of his study: *My son, if you will receive my words and treasure my commandments within you, make your ear attentive to wisdom, incline your heart to understanding; for if you cry for discernment, lift your voice for understanding; if you seek her as silver and search for her as for hidden treasures; then you will discern the fear of the LORD and discover the knowledge of God* (Proverbs 2:1-5).

Seeking for silver and searching for hidden treasures means hard work, and the person who wants to get not only the silver, but the gold as well, out of the Bible, and find its hidden treasures, must make up his mind to dig. It is not merely glancing at the Word or reading the Word that produces the greatest results, but studying the Word, meditating upon the Word, and pondering the Word.

The reason why many get so little out of their Bible reading is simply because they are not willing to think. Intellectual laziness lies at the bottom of a large percent of fruitless Bible reading. People are constantly crying for new methods of Bible study, but what many of them want is simply some method of Bible study by which they can get all the good out of the Bible without work. If someone could tell lazy Christians some method of Bible study by which they could put the sleepiest ten minutes of the day into Bible study, and still get the profit out of it that God intends His children to get out of the study of His Word, that would be just what they desire. But it can't be done. People must be willing to work – and to work hard – if they want to dig out the treasures of infinite wisdom and knowledge and blessing that He has stored up in His Word.

A business friend once asked me in a hurried call to tell him "in a word" how to study his Bible. I replied, "Think." The psalmist pronounces that person "blessed" who meditates in the law of the Lord day and night. *How blessed is the man who does not walk in the counsel of the wicked, nor stand in the path of sinners, nor sit in the seat of scoffers! But his delight is in the law of the LORD, and in His law he meditates day and night* (Psalm 1:1-2). The Lord commanded Joshua to *meditate on it day and night,* assuring him that as a result of this meditation, *then you will make your way prosperous, and then you will have success* (Joshua 1:8).

Of Mary, the mother of Jesus, we read, *Mary treasured all these things, pondering them in her heart* (Luke 2:19). In this way alone can one study the Bible to the greatest profit. A half pound of beef well chewed and digested and absorbed will give more strength than tons of beef merely glanced at. One verse of Scripture chewed and digested and absorbed will give more strength than whole chapters simply skimmed. Weigh every word you read in the Bible. Look at it. Turn it over and over. The most familiar passages get a new meaning in this way. Spend fifteen minutes on each word in Psalm 23:1 or Philippians 4:19, for example, and see if it is not so.

The fourth condition is a will wholly surrendered to God. Jesus said, *If anyone is willing to do His will, he will know of the teaching* (John 7:17). A surrendered will gives that clearness of spiritual vision that is necessary to understand God's Book. Many of the difficulties and obscurities of the Bible rise entirely from the fact that the will of the student is not surrendered to the will of the Author of the Book. It is remarkable how passages that once puzzled us become clear and simple and beautiful when we are brought to that place where we say to God, "I surrender my will unconditionally to Yours. I have no will but Your will. Teach me Your will."

A will surrendered to God will do more to make the Bible an open book than a university education. It is simply impossible to get the most profit out of your Bible study until you surrender your will to God. You must be very definite about this. There are many who say, "Oh, yes, I think my will is surrendered to God," yet it is not. They have never gone alone with God and said intelligently and definitely to Him, "O God, I here and now give myself up to You, for You to command me, lead me, shape me, send me, and do with me completely as You want." Such an act is a wonderful key to unlock the treasure house of God's Word. The Bible becomes a new book to the person who sincerely does that. Doing that brought about a complete transformation in my own theology and life and ministry.

The fifth condition is very closely related to the fourth. **The student of the Bible who wants to get the most profit out of his studies must be obedient to its teachings as soon as he sees them.** It was good advice that James gave to early Christians, and to us: *Prove yourselves doers of the word, and not merely hearers who delude themselves* (James 1:22). There are many people who consider themselves Bible students who are deceiving themselves in this way today. They see what the Bible teaches, but they do not do it, and they soon lose their power to see it. Truth obeyed leads to more truth. Truth disobeyed destroys the capacity for discovering truth.

There must be not only a general surrender of the will, but specific practical obedience to each new word of God discovered. There is no place where the law is more joyously certain on the one hand and more sternly unyielding on the other than in the matter of using or refusing the truth revealed in the Bible. *For to everyone who has, more shall be given, and he will have an abundance; but from the one who does not have, even what he does have shall be taken away* (Matthew 25:29). Use, and you get more; refuse, and you lose all.

Do not study the Bible for the mere gratification of intellectual curiosity, but study it to find out how to live and to please God. Whatever duty you find commanded in the Bible, do it at once. Whatever good you see in any Bible character, imitate it immediately. Whatever mistake you note in the actions of Bible men and women, scrutinize your own life to see if you are making the same mistake – and if you find that you are, correct it immediately.

James compares the Bible to a mirror. *If anyone is a hearer of the word and not a doer, he is like a man who looks at his natural face in a mirror; for once he has looked at himself and gone away, he has immediately forgotten what kind of person he was* (James 1:23-24). The main benefit of a mirror is to show you if there is anything out of order about you, and if you find that there is, you can set it right. Use the Bible in that way. Obeying the truth you already see will solve the mysteries in the verses you do not as yet understand. Disobeying the truth you see darkens the whole world of truth. This is the secret of much of the skepticism and error of the day. People saw the truth but did not do it, and now it is gone.

I knew a bright and promising young minister who made rapid advancement in the truth. He took very advanced ground upon one important point especially, and the backlash came. Then one day he said to his wife, "It is very nice to believe this, but we do not need to speak so much about it." They began, or he, at least, to hide their testimony. Next his wife died, and sadly, he drifted. The Bible became to him a sealed book. Faith reeled. He publicly renounced his faith in some of the fundamental truths of the Bible. He seemed to lose his grip even on the doctrine of immortality. What was the cause of it all? Truth flees away that is not lived and stood for. That man is much admired and applauded by some today, but daylight has given place to darkness in his soul.

The sixth condition is a childlike mind. God reveals His deepest truths to babes. No age more than our own needs to take to heart the words of Jesus: *I praise You, Father, Lord of heaven and earth, that You have hidden these things from the wise and intelligent and have revealed them to infants* (Matthew 11:25).

In what way must we be infants if God is to reveal His truth to us and we are to understand His Word? A child is not full of his own wisdom. He recognizes his ignorance and is ready to be taught. He does not stand on his own notions and ideas in opposition to those of his teachers. It is in that spirit that we should come to the Bible if we want to get the most profit out of our study.

Do not come to the Bible full of your own ideas, trying to get confirmation of them. Come rather to find out what God's ideas are as He has revealed them there. Do not come to find a confirmation of your own opinion, but come to be taught what God will be pleased to teach. If a person comes to the Bible just to find his own ideas taught there, he will find them; but if he comes recognizing his own ignorance, just as a little child, and to be taught, he will find something infinitely better than his own ideas – even the mind of God.

We see why many people cannot see things that are plainly taught in the Bible. The doctrine taught in the Bible is not their own idea or belief, and they are so full of their own beliefs, ideas, and traditions that they have no room left for what the Bible actually teaches. We have an illustration of this in the apostles themselves at one stage in their training. In Mark 9:31 we read that *He was teaching His disciples and telling them, "The Son of Man is to be delivered into the hands of men, and they will kill Him; and when He has been killed, He will rise three days later."* Now that is as plain and definite as language can make it, but it was utterly contrary to the notions of the apostles as to what was to happen to the Christ. So we read in the next verse that *they did not understand this statement* (Mark 9:32). Is that not amazing? But is it any more reason to be amazed than our own inability to comprehend plain statements in the Bible when they run counter to our preconceived notions?

The difficulties that many Christians find with portions of the Sermon on the Mount would be plain enough if we just came to Christ like a child to be taught what to believe and do, rather than coming as fully grown adults who already know it all and who must find some interpretations of Christ's words that will fit into our mature and infallible philosophy.

Many people are so full of unbiblical theology they have been taught that it takes them a lifetime to get rid of it and to understand the clear teaching of the Bible. "Oh, what can this verse mean?" many bewildered people cry. It means what it plainly says; but what you are after is not the meaning God has plainly put into it, but the meaning you can twist and try to make fit by some ingenious trick of exegesis into your own ideas and schemes. Don't come to the Bible to find out what you can make it mean, but come to the Bible to find out what God intended it to mean.

People often miss the real truth of a verse by saying, "But that can be interpreted this way." Oh, yes, maybe it can be, but is that the way God intended it to be interpreted? If we want to get the most profit out of our Bible study, we need to pray often, "Oh, God, make me a little child. Empty me of my own notions. Teach me Your own mind. Make me ready like a little child to receive all that You have to say, no matter how contrary it is to what I have thought and believed before." How the Bible opens up to one who approaches it in that way! How it closes up to the wise fool who thinks he knows everything and imagines he can give points to Peter and Paul, and even to Jesus Christ and to God Himself! Someone has well said that the best method of Bible study is "the baby method."

I was once talking with a ministerial friend about what seemed to be the clear teaching of a certain passage. "Yes," he replied, "but that doesn't agree with my philosophy." This man was sincere, yet, sadly, he did not have the childlike spirit that is an essential condition of the most profitable Bible study. But there are many who approach the Bible in the same way. It is a great point gained in Bible study when we are brought to realize that an infinite God knows more than we do, that indeed our highest wisdom is less than the knowledge of the most ignorant child compared with His. Let us come to Him as babes, just to be taught by Him and not to argue with Him. But we so easily and so constantly forget this, that every time we open our Bibles, we would do well to get down humbly before God and say, "Father, I am only a child. Teach me."

The seventh condition of studying the Bible to the greatest profit is that we study it as the Word of God. The apostle Paul, in writing to the church of the Thessalonians, thanked God without ceasing that when they received the Word of God, they *accepted it not as the word of men, but for what it really is, the word of God* (1 Thessalonians 2:13). Paul could rightly thank God for that, and we can rightly thank God when we get to the place where we receive the Word of God as *the word of God.*

This does not mean that someone who does not believe that the Bible is the Word of God should be discouraged from studying it. Indeed, one of the best things one who does not believe that the Bible is the Word of God can do, if he is honest, is to study it. I once completely doubted that the Bible was the Word of God, and the firm confidence that I have today that the Bible is the Word of God has come more from the study of the Book itself than from anything else. Those who doubt it are more often those who study about the Bible than those who dig into the actual teachings of the Book itself.

But while the best book of Christian evidences is the Bible, and while the most complete skeptic should be encouraged to study it, we will not get the most profit out of that study until we reach the point where we become convinced that the Bible is God's Word, and when we study it as such. There is a great difference between believing theoretically that the Bible is God's Word and studying it as God's Word. Thousands of people would tell you that they believe the Bible is God's Word – who do not study it as God's Word.

Studying the Bible as the Word of God involves four things:

First, it involves the unquestioning acceptance of its teachings when they are obviously seen, even when they may appear unreasonable or impossible. Reason demands that we submit our judgment and reasonings to the statements of infinite wisdom. There is nothing more irrational than rationalism, which makes finite wisdom the test of infinite wisdom and submits the teachings of God's omniscience to the approval of man's judgment. It is the most extreme and absurd conceit that says, "This cannot be true, even though God says it, for it does not approve itself to *my* reason." *On the contrary, who are you, O man, who answers back to God?* (Romans 9:20). Real human wisdom, when it finds infinite wisdom, bows before it and says, "Speak what you will, and I will believe."

Once we have become convinced that the Bible is God's Word, its teachings must be the end of all controversy and discussion. *Thus saith the* LORD will settle every question. There are many people who profess to believe that the Bible is the Word of God, but if you show them what the Bible clearly teaches on some disputed point, they will shake their heads and say, "Yes, but *I think* so and so," or "Doctor, or Professor this, or our church doesn't teach that way." There is little profit in that sort of Bible study.

Studying the Bible as the Word of God involves, in the second place, absolute reliance upon all its promises in all their length and breadth. The person who studies the Bible as the Word of God will not discount any one of its promises one bit. The one who studies the Bible as the Word of God will say, "God, who cannot lie, has promised" (Titus 1:2). He will not try to make God a liar by trying to make one of His promises mean less than it says.

The one who studies the Bible as the Word of God will be on the lookout for promises, and as soon as he finds one, he will seek to discover just what it means; and as soon as he discovers what it means, he will step right out upon that promise and will risk everything upon its full meaning.

That is one of the secrets of profitable Bible study. Hunt for promises and appropriate them as fast as you find them. This is done by meeting the conditions and risking all upon them. That is the way to make your own all the fullness of blessing God has for you. This is the key to all the treasures of God's grace. Happy is the person who has so learned to study the Bible as God's Word that he is ready to claim for himself every new promise as it appears, and to risk everything upon it.

Studying the Bible as the Word of God involves, in the third place, obedience – prompt, exact obedience, without asking any questions – to its every precept. Obedience may seem difficult or even impossible, but God has required it, and I must simply obey and leave the results with God. If you want to get the very most profit out of your Bible study, resolve that from this time forward you will claim every clear promise and obey every plain command, and that as to the promises and commands whose meaning is not yet clear, you will try to get their meaning made clear.

In the fourth place, studying the Bible as the Word of God involves studying it as in God's presence. When you read a verse of Scripture, hear the voice of the living God speaking directly to you in those written words. There is new power and attractiveness in the Bible when you have learned to hear a living, present person – God, our Father, Himself – talking directly to you in these words.

One of the most fascinating and inspiring statements

in the Bible is *Enoch walked with God* (Genesis 5:24). We can have God's glorious companionship any moment we please by simply opening His Word and letting the living and ever-present God speak to us through it. With what holy awe and extraordinary and unutterable joy one studies the Bible if he studies it in this way! It is heaven come down to earth.

The eighth and last condition of the most profitable Bible study is prayerfulness. The psalmist prayed, *Open my eyes, that I may behold wonderful things from Your law* (Psalm 119:18). Everyone who desires to get the most profit out of his Bible study needs to offer that or a similar prayer every time he undertakes the study of the Word. Few keys open as many boxes that contain hidden treasure as prayer. Few clues unravel as many difficulties. Few microscopes will disclose as many beauties hidden from the eye of the ordinary observer.

What new light often shines from an old familiar text as you bend over it in prayer! I believe in studying the Bible a good deal on your knees. When one reads an entire book through upon his knees – and this is easily done – that book has a new meaning and becomes a new book. One ought never to open the Bible to read it without at least lifting the heart to God in silent prayer that He will interpret it and illumine its pages by the light of His Spirit. It is a rare privilege to study any book under the immediate guidance and instruction of its author, and this is the privilege of us all in studying the Bible.

When one comes to a passage that is difficult to understand or difficult to interpret, instead of ignoring it or rushing to some learned friend or to some commentary, he should lay that passage before God and ask Him to explain it to him, pleading God's promise: *If any of you lacks wisdom, let him ask of God, who gives to all generously and without reproach, and it will be given to him. But he must ask in faith without any doubting* (James 1:5-6). It is simply wonderful how the seemingly most difficult passages become plain in this way.

Harry Morehouse, one of the most remarkable Bible scholars among uneducated men, used to say that whenever he came to a passage in the Bible that he could not understand, he would search through the Bible for some other passage that threw light upon it, and then lay it before God in prayer. He said that he had never found a passage that did not yield to this treatment.

I have had quite a similar experience. Some years ago I was with a friend touring the Franconian Switzerland and visiting some of the more famous underground caves. One day the country letter carrier stopped us and asked if we would like to see a cave of rare beauty and interest, away from the beaten tracks of travel. Of course, we said yes. He led us through the woods and underbrush to the mouth of the cave, and we entered. All was dark and uncanny. He spoke much about the beauty of the cave, telling us of altars and fantastic formations, but we could see absolutely nothing. Now and then he uttered a note to warn us to be careful, as near our feet lay a gulf, the bottom of which had never been discovered. We began to fear that we might be the first discoverers of the bottom. There was nothing pleasant about the whole affair. But as soon as a torch was lit, everything became different. There were the stalagmites rising from the floor to meet the stalactites as they came down from the ceiling. There were beautiful and fantastic formations on every hand, and all glistening in the light.

I have often thought it was like that with many passages of Scripture. Others tell you of its beauty, but you cannot see it. It looks dark and intricate and forbidding and dangerous, but when God's own light is kindled there by prayer, how different all becomes in an instant. You see a beauty that language cannot express, and that only those who have stood there in the same light can appreciate.

He who would understand and love his Bible must be much in prayer. Prayer will do more than a college education to make the Bible an open and glorious book. Perhaps the best lesson I learned in a German university, where I had the privilege of receiving the instruction of one of the most noted and most gifted Bible teachers of any age, was that which came through the statement of the assistant of this professor, that Professor Franz Delitzsch worked out much of his teaching upon his knees.

Chapter 9

Final Suggestions

There are some suggestions that remain to be given before we close this book.

Study the Bible daily. Consistency counts for more in Bible study than most people think. The occasional student, who at certain seasons gives a great deal of time to the study of the Word, and at other seasons quite neglects it, even for days at a time, does not achieve the results that he does who plods on regularly day by day. The Bereans were wise as well as *noble-minded* in that they examined *the Scriptures daily* (Acts 17:11).

A man who is well known among the Christian college students of America once remarked at a student convention that he had been at many conventions and had received great blessings from them, but the greatest blessing he had ever received was from a convention where there were only four people gathered together. The blessing had come to him in this way. These four had covenanted together to spend a certain part of every day in Bible study. Since that day, much of his time had been spent traveling or in hotels and at conventions, but he had tried to keep that covenant, and the greatest blessing that had come to him in his Christian life had come through this daily study of the Word.

No one who has not tried it realizes how much can be accomplished by setting apart a specific part of each day for Bible study, and keeping it sacredly for that purpose under all circumstances. It might not be more than fifteen or thirty minutes, but it certainly should be an hour. Many will say that they do not have the time. It will be time saved. Lord Cairns, one of the busiest as well as most eminent men of his day, testified before his death that his first two hours of every day were given to the study of the Bible and prayer, and he attributed the great achievements of his life to that fact.

It will not do to study the Bible only when we feel like it. It will not do to study the Bible only when we have spare time. We must have firm principles and habits in this matter if we are to study the Bible to the greatest profit. Nothing that we do will be more important than our Bible study, and it cannot give way to other less important things. What regularity in eating is to physical life, regularity in Bible study is to spiritual life. Set some time, even if it is no more than fifteen minutes to start with, and keep to it until you are ready to set a longer period.

Select for your Bible study the best part of the day that you can give to it. Do not put your Bible study off until nearly bedtime, when the mind is drowsy. It is good to take a parting verse for the day when one goes to bed for the night, but this is not the time for study. No study demands all that there is in a person as much as Bible study does. Do not take the time immediately after a heavy meal. The mind is more or less sluggish after a heavy meal, and it is unwise to put it to hard work then. It is almost the unanimous opinion of those who have given this subject careful attention that the early hours of the day are the best for Bible study, if they can be secured free from interruption. It is good, whenever possible, to lock yourself in and lock the world out when you are about to give yourself up to the study of the Bible.

In all your Bible study, look for Christ in the passage under examination. We read of Jesus that *beginning with Moses and with all the prophets, He explained to them the things concerning Himself in all the Scriptures* (Luke 24:27). Jesus Christ is the subject of the whole Bible, and the subject permeates the entire Book. Some of the seemingly driest portions of the Bible become filled with new life when we learn to see Christ in them.

I remember in my early reading of the Bible what a dull book Leviticus seemed to be, but it all became different when I learned to see Jesus in the various offerings and sacrifices, in the high priest and his garments, in the tabernacle and its furniture – indeed, everywhere. Look for Christ in every verse you study, and even the genealogies and lists of the names of towns will begin to have beauty and power.

Memorize Scripture. The psalmist said, *Your word I have treasured in my heart, that I may not sin against You* (Psalm 119:11). There is nothing better to keep one from sinning than this. By the Word of God laid up in His heart, Jesus overcame the tempter (Matthew 4:4, 7, 10).

The Word of God laid up in the heart is good for purposes other than victory over sin. It is good to meet and expose error. It is good to enable one *to sustain the weary one with a word* (Isaiah 50:4). It is good for many uses, even *that the man of God may be adequate, equipped for every good work* (2 Timothy 3:17).

Memorize Scripture by chapter and verse. It is quite as easy as merely memorizing the words, and it is immeasurably more useful for practical purposes. Memorize the Scripture in systematic form. Do not have a chaotic heap of texts in the mind, but categorize under appropriate titles the verses you store in memory. Then you can bring them out when you need them without racking your brains. There are many men who can stand up without a moment's warning and talk coherently, articulately, and scripturally on any vital theme because they have a vast collection of wisdom in the form of Scripture texts stored away in their minds in systematic form.

Finally, make practical use of spare moments in the study of the Bible. In most people's lives there is a vast amount of wasted time – time spent in traveling, time spent in waiting for people with whom they have appointments, time spent in waiting for meals, etc. Most of this can be used for the study of the Bible, if you carry with you a pocket Bible or pocket New Testament. You can also use this time to meditate upon texts stored away in your memory. Many of my sermons and speeches are worked out in this way.

It is said that Henry Ward Beecher read one of the larger histories of England through while waiting day after day for his meals to be brought to the table. How many books of the Bible could be studied in the same time? A friend once told me that the man who had, in some respects, the most extraordinary knowledge of the Bible of anyone he knew, was a junk dealer in a Canadian city. This man had a Bible open on his shelves, and during intervals of business he would meditate on the Word of God. The Bible became very black by being handled in such surroundings, but I have little doubt his soul became correspondingly white. There is no management of resources that pays as well as does management of time, and there is no way of making use of time as wisely as putting the moments that are going to waste into the study of or meditation upon the Word of God.

Reuben A. Torrey
– A Brief Biography

Reuben A. Torrey was an author, conference speaker, pastor, evangelist, Bible college dean, and more. Torrey was born in Hoboken, New Jersey, on January 28, 1856. He graduated from Yale University in 1875 and from Yale Divinity School in 1878, when he became the pastor of a Congregational church in Garrettsville, Ohio. Torrey married Clara Smith in 1879, with whom he had five children.

In 1882, he went to Germany, where he studied at the universities at Leipzig and Erlangen. Upon returning to the United States, Torrey pastored in Minneapolis, and was also in charge of the Congregational City Mission Society. In 1889, Dwight L. Moody called upon Torrey to lead his Chicago Evangelization Society, which later became the Moody Bible Institute. Beginning in 1894, Torrey was also the pastor of the Chicago Avenue Church, which was later called the Moody Memorial Church. He was a chaplain with the YMCA during the Spanish-American War, and was also a chaplain during World War I.

Torrey traveled all over the world leading evangelistic tours, preaching to the unsaved. It is believed that more than one hundred thousand were saved under his preaching. In 1908, he helped start the Montrose Bible Conference in Pennsylvania, which continues today. He became dean of the Bible Institute of Los Angeles (now Biola University) in 1912, and was the pastor of the Church of the Open Door in Los Angeles from 1915 to 1924.

Torrey continued speaking all over the world and holding Bible conferences. He died in Asheville, North Carolina, on October 26, 1928.

Torrey was a very active evangelist and soul winner, speaking to people everywhere he went, in public and in private, about their souls, seeking to lead the lost to Jesus. He authored more than forty books, including *How to Bring Men to Christ, How to Pray, How to Study the Bible for Greatest Profit, How to Obtain Fullness of Power in Christian Life and Service*, and *Why God Used D. L. Moody*, and also helped edit the twelve-volume book about the fundamentals of the faith, titled *The Fundamentals*. He was also known as a man of prayer, and his teaching, preaching, writing, and his entire life proved that he walked closely with God.

Other Similar Titles

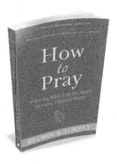

How to Pray, by Reuben A. Torrey

It is not necessary that the whole church prays to begin with. Great revivals always begin first in the hearts of a few men and women whom God arouses by His Spirit to believe in Him as a living God, as a God who answers prayer, and upon whose heart He lays a burden from which no rest can be found except in persistent crying unto God.

May God use this book to inspire many who are currently prayerless, or nearly so, to pray earnestly. May God stir up your own heart to be one of those burdened to pray, and to pray until God answers.

Available where books are sold.

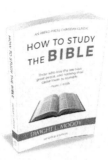

How to Study the Bible, by Dwight L. Moody

There is no situation in life for which you cannot find some word of consolation in Scripture. If you are in affliction, if you are in adversity and trial, there is a promise for you. In joy and sorrow, in health and in sickness, in poverty and in riches, in every condition of life, God has a promise stored up in His Word for you.

This classic book by Dwight L. Moody brings to light the necessity of studying the Scriptures, presents methods which help stimulate excitement for the Scriptures, and offers tools to help you comprehend the difficult passages in the Scriptures. To live a victorious Christian life, you must read and understand what God is saying to you. Moody is a master of using stories to illustrate what he is saying, and you will be both inspired and convicted to pursue truth from the pages of God's Word.

Available where books are sold.

The Pursuit of God, by A. W. Tozer

To have found God and still to pursue Him is a paradox of love, scorned indeed by the too-easily-satisfied religious person, but justified in happy experience by the children of the burning heart. Saint Bernard of Clairvaux stated this holy paradox in a musical four-line poem that will be instantly understood by every worshipping soul:

> *We taste Thee, O Thou Living Bread,*
> *And long to feast upon Thee still:*
> *We drink of Thee, the Fountainhead*
> *And thirst our souls from Thee to fill.*

Come near to the holy men and women of the past and you will soon feel the heat of their desire after God. Let A. W. Tozer's pursuit of God spur you also into a genuine hunger and thirst to truly know God.

Available where books are sold.

Pilgrim's Progress, by John Bunyan

Often disguised as something that would help him, evil accompanies Christian on his journey to the Celestial City. As you walk with him, you'll begin to identify today's many religious pitfalls. These are presented by men such as Pliable, who turns back at the Slough of Despond; and Ignorance, who believes he's a true follower of Christ when he's really only trusting in himself. Each character represented in this allegory is intentionally and profoundly accurate in its depiction of what we see all around us, and unfortunately, what we too often see in ourselves. But while Christian is injured and nearly killed, he eventually prevails to the end. So can you.

Available where books are sold.

Absolute Surrender, by Andrew Murray

God waits to bless us in a way beyond what we expect. From the beginning, ear has not heard, neither has the eye seen, what God has prepared for those who wait for Him (Isaiah 64:4). God has prepared unheard of things, things you never can think of, blessings much more wonderful than you can imagine and mightier than you can conceive. They are divine blessings. Oh, come at once and say, "I give myself absolutely to God, to His will, to do only what God wants." God will enable you to carry out the surrender necessary, if you come to Him with a sincere heart.

Available where books are sold.

Holiness, by J. C. Ryle

Practical holiness and entire self-consecration to God are not given adequate attention by modern Christians. The unsaved sometimes rightly complain that Christians are not as kind and unselfish and good-natured as those who make no profession of faith. Far too many Christians make a verbal proclamation of faith, yet remain unchanged in heart and lifestyle. But Scripture makes it clear that holiness, in its place and proportion, is quite as important as justification. Holiness, without which no one shall see the Lord (Hebrews 12:14). It is imperative that Christians are biblically and truly holy.

Available where books are sold.

Made in the USA
Coppell, TX
27 April 2022

77106459R00077